Cat Questions
and Answers

Cat Questions and Answers

*A handbook of helpful
and curious advice for
cats and their owners*

*Compiled by
Celia Haddon*

Robinson
IN COLLABORATION WITH
THE DAILY TELEGRAPH

Robinson Publishing Ltd
7 Kensington Church Court
London W8 4SP

A copy of the British Library Cataloguing in Publication Data
for this title is available from the British Library

ISBN 1–84119–045–4

Illustrations by Ken Cox
Printed and bound in Finland by WSOY

Contents

Devoted Owners and Cats who Dominate Them

Cats are my obsession. My waking hours are punctuated by feline duties – opening the door for them when they want to go out; shutting the door for them when they change their minds; opening it again as they change their minds again; feeding them little snacks at odd hours; buying mineral water for them because they don't like tap water; trying to stop them walking on my computer keyboard; brushing and combing them; kissing their foreheads; giving (or trying to give) them worm pills; cleaning their litter trays twice a day; moving over in the bed at night when they join me under the duvet; being woken as they walk up and down my sleeping body when they think it's breakfast time; playing with bits of string . . .

Daily Telegraph readers' letters have proved that I am not alone in being cat mad. Wonderfully devoted letters have flowed in from readers who let their cats sleep on the bed at night (sometimes between husband and wife), others who uncomplainingly clear up after incontinent elderly cats, and people who get used to being woken up in the morning by cats biting their toes under the duvet or falling on them from a great height.

There are people who take their cats for walks, thoughtfully pausing in the bitter cold as the cat examines hedgerows or climbs halfway up a tree. Others fill their living rooms with gigantic cat aerobic centres from floor to ceiling, or purchase special wildlife videos for their cats to enjoy watching. We will put up with a lot – spraying on the best curtains, scratching the wallpaper, tearing the chairs to shreds, draughts through the cat flap, the smell of the litter tray, and the best armchairs occupied by cats who make it clear there is no space for humans.

For in many ways cats seem to have the upper paw. True, we humans are the ones who choose and buy the cat food. But set against this is the undeniable fact that cats train us to bring home the cat food they prefer, usually the most expensive variety.

Cats have immense ingenuity in solving what they see as a problem – far greater ingenuity, alas, than their human owners show! For my official job is to try to find solutions to cat owners' problems. Human problems are not feline ones. Smell, mess, and feline urine are often ingenious feline solutions to what a cat sees as a problem.

I am often surprised at how long owners will put up with almost intolerable behaviour (in human terms) from their cats. If the cats are scent-marking the house as a way of making themselves feel better, their owners will tolerate the smell of cat urine for months. Many of the people who write to me have been putting up with it for a year or more, feeling the same kind of shyness and shame that are common among sufferers from the more embarrassing human social diseases! They writhe under the misconception that they are the only person with the problem. To all those who have difficulties with their cats I would like to say that you are not alone. There are literally tens of thousands of households which smell of cat's pee at some time or other and probably millions of us whose armchair coverings are hanging in shreds!

The other mental block which stops people getting help is the feeling that they should be able to solve the problem with discipline. Usually there is somebody, a neighbour or a "friend", who tells them they should punish their cats – for our society still permits the disciplining of animals (and alas, children) by hitting them. We raise our voices and we cause the animal pain, in the hope that the animal will learn its lesson.

It doesn't, of course. Why should it? It doesn't understand what we say to it and usually the punishment is administered minutes, sometimes hours, after the problematic behaviour has ceased. All that the cat learns is that this human being will occasionally and unpredictably hit it. Indeed, most cat difficulties will be intensified by any kind of punishment.

Luckily people who write to me are not the punishing kind. They are indulgent, loving, passionately caring owners. And in their loving households, cats blossom into their true selves. One of the delights of opening my letters is the realization that I am not alone in being cat obsessed. Every post bag is therapy for me!

Sometimes I can help owners with their feline dilemmas. Some solutions come from other readers who write in with spectacularly ingenious ideas. Friendly vets have advised me; rescue and advice organizations have helped; so have many cat behaviour counsellors. The best advice in this book comes from others; I have merely set it down.

Those of you with difficult cats may find help here. There is a list of experts at the back of this book, including cat behaviour counsellors and vets who have a special interest in cats, and other sources of help. I have also tried to list some of the products that seem useful, though no doubt I have missed many good things.

But the problems in this book are only part of it. Many letters cast interesting light on the human–cat relationship and these I have run without answers. The letters in this first chapter come from people whose cats are very firmly in charge. They didn't need answers from me, because clearly the owners enjoy being cat slaves! I invite you to enjoy the rich eccentricity of this particular relationship . . .

Tubby Tabby in Bed

Tubby Tabby is our pet name for my giant tabby, Tiggy. He likes to sit near me at all times, whether I am writing, stripping the wallpaper or painting (we have just moved into a new house). He never gets in the way, and when told not to touch something, he gives me that look to show that he has understood, and stays away from the forbidden object. He sleeps with us, head on the pillow between my husband and me, for all the world like a small human being. He sleeps right through until we get up, sometimes as late as nine o'clock, and never disturbs us by kneading or asking for food.

C.W., Shepperton, Middlesex

On-line Cat

As a besotted cat owner I would like to report that when I was on holiday in Ireland, I phoned home and got my husband to call Tiddly-widdly-widdly, my grey cat. By a miracle she came, and while I shouted messages like "I'll be back soon, T.W.W.", she licked the phone all over in her excitement.

C.R., Geneva, Italy

Posh Names

Our cat, Hazel, is a tabby-and-white with ginger bits and a striped brown-and-white tail, a rescue cat. As the new loving owner, I rang the vet's to ask about injections. I must have made a fuss because on arrival at the surgery, the receptionist, about to register my cat, peered into her box and said "She's only a moggie" and waved the file card at me. Quick as a flash, outraged to my core, my reply was: "That card is not big enough. This cat is called Little Princess, Hazel Honeybunch, Thunder Paws Richardson." The poor receptionist, a victim of the roars of laughter from a packed surgery, duly typed the card and asked if it would do. Immediately I spotted that she had missed out the aitch in Thunder Paws, and said so, whereupon the whole card was retyped!

G.R., Barnsley, South Yorkshire

Armchair Manipulation

Hillary seems to be a prime candidate for the Ingenious Methods of Getting One's Own Way award for cats. She has devised a way of getting a chair to sleep on. She likes it warmed, so she gets up on someone's knee (usually my husband's), sits there until she thinks the chair is warm enough, then pushes down at the side of him to get him off. If that is the chair she wants, well and good. She curls contentedly and settles to sleep. If not, she hopes that, having driven him off one chair, he will sit where she really wants to be. The sitting-on-knee-tipping-off-chair routine is then repeated, resulting in her getting her own way.

M.G., Nuneaton, Warwickshire

Jake and Laps

I am writing to include my Abyssinian, Jake, as a candidate for bullying cat – though I personally think that bullying is their intelligent way to communicate their needs. His latest trick is when jumping up on my lap. If my legs are crossed, he will push his head at the offending knee until I uncross them to make a flat lap for him.

H.W., Southport, Lancashire

5

Susie the Scratcher

Susie wants what she wants and she wants it now. If at the front of the house, she stands on her hind legs and scratches furiously at the door (which is wooden). She has made a noticeable deep gash. She tears into the parlour and scratches the furniture until food is supplied. If it is not to her liking, this action will be repeated. If she is put outside, she immediately runs to the back of our house (some way from the front since we are in a terrace block) and scratches the French windows. On summer days she sits on the front wall waiting for assorted neighbours to pay her some attention. She is much admired by these people, but little do they know what a tyrant she can be indoors.

V.G., West London

Persistent Chloe

Our sixteen-year-old cat, Chloe, is a bully in the nicest possible way. She hates us reading if she's in the mood for some attention. At first she will nudge the book with her nose and, if that gets no response, she will push her head up under the book and on to my chest, where she will rub her nose against mine to stop me reading. Then, if I push her down on to my lap, she will try the long route up over the back of the chair on to my shoulder and down on to my chest, where she will sit purring loudly and blocking my view of the page. It's very effective and she always gets her own way. I give in and end up making a fuss of her.

J.W., Andover, Hampshire

Compulsive Groomer

Bianca, a black-and-white shorthair, was a compulsive groomer. She would hold her brother in a vice-like grip and lick him with rapid ferocity. Any resistance was met with a fight, which she usually won. She included my husband in this highly autocratic ritual by sitting on the top of the armchair each evening and holding his head in the same iron grasp, while flattening his hair down on to his scalp very purposefully with her tongue. It was unhygienic but we were too fascinated to stop her. She applied the same ruthless efficiency to waking us up, by meowing loudly. If my husband failed to respond, she would pat his face with her paw. Failing this she would bite him. One day she bit his bottom and he had to have a tetanus jab.

W.G., Bolton, Lancashire

Wake-up Calls

Vashti, our half-Siamese tortoiseshell, has perfected a fail-safe system for getting us out of bed when she requires breakfast. Her methods are wide and varied, and operate on an escalating scale of pain or irritation until one of us is forced out of bed. The attack commences with a *sotto voce* murmur. Having selected the victim for the morning she settles herself beside the victim's ear and purrs loudly.

At this point her methods diverge. For Steve, she looks to see how deeply he is asleep by pulling up his eyelid by the lashes to open an eye. When he had a moustache, this would get tweaked. If he turns over, she starts kneading on the back/neck area until the pain drives him out of bed. Should this fail, desperation measures involve clambering up via the drapes to the half tester over the bed and launching herself some six feet on to his solar plexus. We considered this wildly funny when she was an eleven-ounce kitten, but at ten-plus pounds the damage is considerable.

For me the torture is more subtle. She jumps to the dressing table, stands on hind legs, and scratches at the mirror as though digging through it. The noise is a bit like chalk on a blackboard. Her last resort is then to climb inside a seven-foot weeping fig plant, my pride and joy, and rattle it vigorously, sending down a shower of leaves and threatening to break the branches off.

J.W., Newark, Nottinghamshire

When she decides it is time for us to get up, Tabby howls in the bedrooms, opens the curtain, then leaps from the windowsill on to the bed, where she walks on top of us. If this does not get us up, she stands on the bed headboard and drops on to the pillow. My wife is normally the one who succumbs first and goes downstairs to make the breakfast. When this is ready she calls up and I have approximately one minute to respond, failing which, Tabby charges upstairs. She stands on her hind legs, lifts up the duvet with her head, and stabs her paw complete with claws into my foot. If she is in a bad mood then she bites my foot.

D.G., Cheadle, Cheshire

Our tortoiseshell cat Lucy favours a slightly different tactic when it comes to rousing us in the morning for her breakfast. After ripping up the bedding and stamping hard all over us, she will then crouch on my chest facing south, her little fat bottom resting against my chin, tail straight out behind her which she then swishes from side to side over my face. Her breakfast speedily follows, though I'm put off mine!

G.K., North London

Door Ritual

My husband and I are well and truly under the paw of Cleo, our eight-year-old Abyssinian. If she decides to go out in the early hours, she yells, jumps on us and clouts us with her paw. Then there is the ritual of which door she is going out of. She will march to the front door and have a look outside, then turn her back and we go to the back door. I have tried to put her out, but she is so quick she has turned round and is in again before I can get the door closed. This front door/back door ritual can be repeated several times a day.

On warm summer nights she likes to stay out. She has a cat flap into the laundry and a comfortable basket there, but, no, she stands under our open bedroom window and yells her head off. The noise is such we have to get up and let her in before our neighbours complain. In spite of all this we love her dearly.

M.I., Thurnby, Leicestershire

Night Waking

Thomas wakes us most mornings at about 5.30 a.m. with a Burmese wail. These banshee calls continue until we can stand it no longer and one of us gets up. He is to be found in the bathroom asking for the cold tap to be turned on. Obviously water there is better than that in the bowls put out for him. He watches the water and, perhaps, drinks a few drops, looks up with a feline smirk on his face and all is quiet again. We have tried closing the bathroom door but the noise is even worse! This has only started over the last few months. Where have we gone wrong, or do we love him to destruction?

M.O., Oxford

Lottie and the Chalet

Lottie wakes me up several times a night. We aren't allowed a cat flap as we are in rented accommodation and if I shut her in a room she tears up the carpet. I put a cardboard box on the front step in the hope that if she went out in the night, she'd stay in it and keep warm. Needless to say she ignored it. Then I hit upon the idea of getting her a proper cat chalet because it would be warmer. I drove fifty miles to a place I heard sold them. I wasn't prepared for how big the chalet was or how expensive. I struggled with three men to fit it in the back of the car. I arrived home and struggled up the garden path with the cat chalet in a wheelbarrow only to find Lottie sitting in the cardboard box. Needless to say it took weeks before she ventured into the cat chalet. She started using it, but after a recent week in a cattery when we went on holiday, she refused to use it again. You will not be surprised to learn that when I took Lottie to my vet to enquire about her behaviour the vet suggested a shrink – not for the cat, you understand, but for me.

B.H., Haslemere, Surrey

P.S.   What I'd really like to know is why a cat that was virtually a stray has such expensive tastes in food. How come she won't eat anything but fresh prawns?

Walking Cats

My eighty-year-old husband not only has had three hip replacements but two years ago had one hip joint completely removed. He feels it essential to take some exercise so, with his Zimmer, each afternoon he walks round our cul-de-sac though on some inclement days he does not feel like it and would not do so without some cat bullying! Kiss, one of our six cats, always accompanies him even in rain, snow and hail. If he is not making a move after lunch she sits in front of him, stares at him and makes it obvious, like a physiotherapist, that she is not impressed by his laziness. She mentally bullies him to get up and go out for some exercise. She always wins so they walk together, very slowly, as she is also old and very arthritic.

C.G., Gravesend, Kent.

I loved the letter about the cat who bullies an eighty-year-old into taking a walk. My lovely husband-to-be had read somewhere that Burmese cats were partial to walking with humans, so when Eilish arrived, he was pleased to test this theory as soon as she was allowed out. I did warn him that he was starting something which he wouldn't be able to stop, and of course for the last three years he has been doing as he's told twice a day, rain or shine, and obediently taken the feline bully wherever *she* wishes to go. He plays hide and seek with her, he waits patiently while she investigates shrubs and holes in the ground, he even climbs trees with her (he's fifty-one years old by the way).

She doesn't walk to heel. He does.

S.M., Brickendonbury, Hertfordshire

Seventy-odd years ago, when I was just a small girl, we used to live at Mount Stuart in property owned by the Marquis of Bute, and used to go to Sunday mass at his private chapel, inside the grounds, roughly one mile from the lodge to the church. Our two cats would accompany us, all the way up to the beautiful church – but seeming to know we were leaving them, they'd disappear into bushes. They emerged as we came out after the service, and would further walk with us to a neighbour's farm for lunch. Climbing into the nearest comfortable chair, utterly exhausted, they'd sleep till we made moves to go home – probably another quarter of a mile. Only then would they make audible mews to ask to be carried!

N.A., Glasgow

We had a two-year-old cat who became a real minder for my elderly father, who at eighty-four was very frail with heart problems. She insisted on walking with him, by his side, tail erect, when he went to get his *Daily Telegraph*. As there was a busy road near the shops, my father would tell Cindy to wait for him, which she used to do. On the way back he just called "Cinders" and she was at his side again, always on the outside of the pavement, seemingly to protect him. She knew my father's routine and would be with him as he put his shoes on, then lead the way to the front door. They would go out together come rain or shine.

J.D., North-west London

Fat Cats, Faddy Cats, Weird Drinking Habits and Compulsive Chewers

Cats are fussy eaters. Country cats can go out hunting and bring back their own food, crunching up fresh mice, whole rabbits and, alas, songbirds. Town cats have to rely on dustbins or learn how to manipulate their owners into buying the right tin. Most of them succeed admirably in doing so. Huge quantities of space in supermarkets are given over to feline delicacies – differently flavoured tins, plastic sachets, dried biscuits, special milk, and treats. Humans may buy the food, but cats make their preferences well known.

Some eating problems are the direct result of our tendency to dote on our cats. One of the fattest cats was Thomas O'Malley who weighed a staggering 16.7 kg. Tiddles, the famous fat cat that lived in the ladies' lavatory in London's Paddington Station in the l970s, weighed in at about 13.6 kg at his fattest. Wobbling from his bed to his food bowl, Tiddles was a sad parody of the grace and beauty of the normal cat. All of the seven women lavatory attendants fed Tiddles, who finally expired from an excess of food. Like them, we owners act as enablers, making it easy for our much-loved feline to put on weight by feeding frequent large meals and sharing food off our own plates. One owner of a gigantically fat cat admitted to me that she and the cat shared a double portion of Balti curry every Saturday night!

How can you tell if your adored feline friend is too fat? Among pedigrees, the tiny Singapura might weigh as little as 1.8 kg without being too thin, while a ragdoll cat could be as heavy as 9 kg without being too fat. But most people have moggies, rather than pedigrees, and the cat's ideal weight will depend on its build.

The first give-away signs of fat are what one vet calls "the little love handles", properly called the inguinal fat pads, which are in the groin area. These swell to produce the saggy abdomen swinging from side to side and the huge expanse of tummy when rolling.

"The easiest way to confirm overweight is to run your fingers over the ribcage," advised Steven Andrews, at the time a vet working on the specialist veterinary diet range of a major pet food manufacturer. "If you can't feel the ribs, you need to take the cat to the vet for a check-up."

Dieting a cat isn't straightforward. One problem facing fat cats' owners is that their cat (if it has a cat flap) may be eating two or even three dinners elsewhere. If so, putting him on a diet may mean keeping him indoors for several weeks. Nor can you bully a cat into eating what he is given. "You can let a dog starve till he eats his dinner, but you can't do this for cats. If they starve, they can suffer from fatty liver disease," says veterinary surgeon Bradley Viner, known for his books on cat care. Because of this, cats who stop eating must have a veterinary check-up urgently. If they go towards their dish, then eat only a mouthful, it may be a sign that they have a sore mouth or a bad tooth. Alternatively, the lack of appetite may be a sign of some other illness.

If a cat is suffering from snuffles, often the legacy of cat flu, its sense of smell and therefore its appetite is impaired. Strong-smelling food, like tinned pilchards in tomato sauce, may tempt them to eat. Lack of appetite can also be the sign of an even more serious illness and occasionally it is the sign of severe depression and stress.

It's also quite common for elderly cats to refuse to eat unless their owner pets them at the same time. Though food is already in the bowl, they will go and fetch their owners specially, waiting for a caress before tucking in. In severe cases of doting owner, a cat may refuse to eat unless the food is given by hand! The surprising thing is not that the cat asks for this attention, but that owners are quite often perfectly happy to fulfil these demands. Some cats go even further, waking up their owners in the middle of the night demanding a snack. Just leaving food for them overnight is not enough.

It is in kittenhood that cats may develop food fads. If they are only fed one kind of food, they may refuse, in adulthood, to eat anything else. A tendency to be finicky about food is also a sign of a pampered cat. When the darling pussycat is slow to eat its food, the loving owner takes away the dish and brings it back full of something more tempting, so the cat learns that a refusal to eat will produce a range of new delicacies.

Tinned cat food has, of course, made feeding a cat very simple, but it has one disadvantage – it is not good for teeth. In the wild a cat's teeth would be kept clean by the effort of crunching up bones and fur. Today, the truly conscientious cat owner will know that cats which are prone to gingivitis need their teeth cleaned regularly, if this is possible!

Some cats have very odd tastes. Fat Ada, one of

mine, used to be mad about garlic sausage, a taste which I attribute to her early years among the dustbins of my rather upmarket street. There are cats who have a passion for asparagus, beetroot, curry, Bombay mix, chocolate, cake, raisins, and even toffees. Another odd characteristic of most cats is the way they prefer drinking water from an absolutely filthy puddle, rather than from their bowl.

Finally, there are cats who insist on chewing unsuitable objects. Siamese and oriental breeds sometimes go in for wool eating and will consume the best part of a sweater in one evening. Other cats start crunching up electric wires, making their owners fear for the safety of the house. Sometimes this is attention-seeking behaviour but often it seems to be a need for crunchy food. After all, moist tinned cat food cannot compare with crunchy fresh mice!

Saggy Tummy

Murphy, our two-year-old female tabby, developed a saggy tummy at the age of about twelve months. She is not at all fat, and the vet says she is fine. She gives the impression that her skin is about five sizes too big for her. I have since noticed the same thing with numerous other tabbies, but never with any other colour cat. Is there an explanation and why should it afflict only tabbies?

M.R., Hexham, Northumberland

It's not just tabbies. I also know of Siamese with saggy tummies, British blues with saggy tummies and moggies of all colours with saggy tummies. John Foster, a vet with a special interest in nutrition, says, "These are flaps of skin running underneath the abdomen, where the fat is deposited in neutered females. Humans go A-shaped in the same way." Breeding queens (female cats) also get saggy tummy but in a different position. They put on sub-mammary fat after kittening."

Neutered toms usually only sag if they get overweight,

while entire toms don't sag at all. Besides, they rarely get fat because they are too busy chasing females, caterwauling and ranging over a huge territory!

More Active Play?

Although my cat isn't grossly overweight (he is about 18-20 lb, I think), he is eleven and not very active so I worry about his health. He has tinned cat food – he'd like about six meals a day but I try to limit him to three – a 400 g tin can last him one-and-a-half days, which is supplemented by some dry food for the less active cat. I haven't bought him any canned diet food from the vet's because it is so expensive. He's still quite playful. Should I encourage active play with string etc.?

C.P., Stoke-on-Trent

Take him to the vet to be weighed and ask for a general health check. The vet can prescribe a slimming diet for him and, with veterinary permission, you can encourage him to do more. Here are some suggestions for energetic games you can play with him.

Fishing-rod pouncing – this allows the owner to be relatively still while the cat chases a toy on the end of a rod and line. Crinkle up a piece of cooking foil and tie it to a thread or string. Pull it up and down stairs with cat in hot pursuit. Buy or make a bundle of feathers and dangle it from the stairs to the cat below, so that the cat jumps up for it.

Buy a cat aerobic centre. This consists of pillars covered with rope cord, with carpet-lined tunnels and platforms sometimes up to ceiling height. The lazy cat will need enticing up the pillars with foil, feathers or fishing-rod!

Refusing the Opened Tin

Pepe, our seventeen-year-old cat, lives mainly on tinned food and eats about half a tin at a session. But although he tackles a newly opened tin with enthusiasm, he firmly refuses to touch the second half and will go hungry all day rather than eat it. We

17

keep open tins covered and in the fridge. Can you suggest anything else we can do?

G.H., St Ives, Cambridgeshire

As cats get old, their taste buds are not so active, says Claire Bessant, an expert on the older cat. "The smell hits you when you open a tin, and it obviously gets through to Pepe too! Take the second half of the tin out of the fridge some time before you offer it to him. Cats don't like cold food. Even try warming it up a little − it should increase the smell."

Refusal to Eat − Trying it on?

Our eleven-year-old cat Sherry started showing signs of holding out on eating her food last November. She would eat just a little, then meow till we gave her something from our plates. We stopped giving her treats, but since then she has been eating even less, sometimes going for days hardly eating at all. We have kept her indoors to ensure she is not being fed by a neighbour. But when the food is put down, she sniffs it and then walks away in disdain. Every other cat owner we have spoken to says she is just being fussy. I waved a raw piece of rabbit in front of her nose and she ate it greedily. This tells me that she is still willing to eat if the food is good enough. Can you confirm that Sherry is taking us for suckers?

P.B., North London

The Feline Advisory Bureau suggest you check for sore teeth or gums. Take her to your vet to have these checked, and while you are there discuss this problem in full detail in case it is something more serious. "Sherry may want to eat, but she knows that it is just too painful. The rabbit may have been tempting enough to make her ignore the pain," says Claire Bessant of the FAB. "Or there may be some underlying illness."

Try warming up her canned food before feeding it, and giving her it piece by piece by hand, to see if you can start her off eating it. Sherry may be holding out for better grub, but even so it is dangerous to let a cat go without food for more than three days. If she is just trying it on, you are going to need to talk to your vet anyway in some detail about what to do next.

Gulpers and Grazers

We have two cats. Tuffy likes to eat a little at a time, coming back to nibble regularly. The other, Biff, gulps all his food down then steals Tuffy's food. As a result we have to keep watch on Tuffy, removing his dish, then re-offering it when he looks hungry. This is obviously not always easy. Have you any solution?

I.S., Tarves, Aberdeenshire

Feline gorgers make life difficult for feline grazers! "Try getting a complete dry food for the second cat, of a kind the first cat doesn't like very much," suggests Sarah White-head, a pet behaviour counsellor. "Feed the first cat a tin of wet food, and leave a large heap of the dry food down for the second cat. With luck the first cat will get bored with eating the dry food."

If the gorging cat is overweight, however, so much food may make him positively obese! In this case, you could try installing a magnetic cat flap within the house leading into the room where you have put the second cat's food. "This can work, but occasionally the greedy cat will learn how to dash in either before or after the flap has opened!" admits Sarah Whitehead. If so, you will just have to go back to careful supervision.

My two cats, Tuppy and Lily, are like Biff and Tuffy. Tuppy is very greedy and gulps everything down including Lily's food if he can. Lily, like Tuffy, is very finicky and eats a small amount and then returns for more later. There is an additional problem in that Tuppy developed cystitis and I have to keep him off dry food completely, while Lily has it for breakfast. I feed her in the kitchen and him in the annexe. If I can't stay in the room to supervise him, I lock the cat flap between the two rooms until Lily has finished. I give her three chances to eat the food, picking it up between times. If I get diverted and have to leave the room, Tuppy will eat it, even if I have put it on the work surface. So I have to put it in a cupboard until Lily decides she has had enough. I am afraid that separate rooms or supervision seem the only answer.

R.M., New Malden, Surrey

Our female cat Tiggy was being driven off her food by her brother, Bertie. My husband devised a dining room for her – a stout cardboard carton with no top and part of one end removed to form a doorway. It was just the right size for Tiggy and her food, and the walls were tall enough to stop Bertie from staring menacingly at her or shouldering her aside. She could eat her meal in comfort and undisturbed.

D.W., Pittenweem, Fife

Picky Cats

Mine is a problem common to many people. Despite the numerous makes and varieties of food available, my two cats, Picketty Witch and Didi, flatly refuse to eat virtually all patent foods and are costing me a fortune as most end up in the dustbin. Both cats are middle-aged. I have tried depriving them of food throughout the day when their breakfast has been spurned, re-offering them the same food for their evening meal, but still it remains uneaten. I am sure they would starve rather than oblige. What am I to do?

E.W., Southport, Lancashire

Cats are expert manipulators. Experience teaches them that if they refuse their food, doting owners will produce something tastier. Start with a high-quality commercial food that your cats will sometimes eat. If you feed a tinned food, then warm it up slightly. Never serve it straight from the fridge.

Start the new diet by offering small portions. If possible, mix the old and new diets, slowly increasing the proportion of the new. If the cats won't eat, take back the food and present it later. Give them small pieces by hand at the start of the meal. Cats should not be starved into a new diet, since more than three days without food can damage their health.

I was very interested by the letter about Picketty Witch and Didi. My two cats do not like eating their food out of the fridge or warmed up. I keep the food in the tin in a cupboard at room temperature and then serve it to them on plates just outside the back door mat. It always works. Whether they think other cats might eat it first, or the fresh air blows away smells, they scoff it up straight away.

S.H., Selsey, West Sussex

Late-night Snacking

Sandy, our three-year-old neutered male cat, has recently been released from quarantine. Before quarantine he was used to being fed his main meals at regular intervals, that is at 6 a.m. (when I got up) and soon after 5 p.m. It was almost as if he could tell the time as he rarely bothered me until a few minutes before the alarm was due to go off. However, he now wakes me up at any time between 4 a.m. and 6.30 a.m. and he persists until I get up and feed him. After another hour or so, he returns and wakes me again for a second helping. He has also learned recently that the gentle application of claws to bare skin gets a quick reaction. Leaving food down has failed as he won't go and look for it on his own. We do not wish to exclude him from the bedroom but would like to know how we can get him to eat at more reasonable times.

M.B., Folkestone, Kent

Sandy is training you very effectively to his new meal times. Every time you give in to him, you are rewarding him for waking you up, so naturally he continues. The problem is not his behaviour but your guilt, which means you cannot bear to say no. Perhaps you feel you have to spoil him after his ordeal in quarantine.

The only way you are going to change his behaviour is to feed him at set times chosen for your (not his) convenience. This means that you must either shut him out of the bedroom, or consistently refuse to respond to his demands. Lie there and do not take any notice of him whatsoever, however difficult this may be.

You will undoubtedly have several mornings without too much sleep and will feel very exhausted. Do not give in. If he starts scratching you, you should shut him out of the bedroom until you get up. Eventually, after a week or two, he will learn that waking you up does not get the reward of food and he will stop doing it.

Bad Gums

When my Siamese kitten, Yindee, was spayed last month – she is now eleven months old – the vet told me she believes Yindee has the start of gingivitis. She advised that I give her dried food, as well as fresh, so she would chew, also small dog biscuits. My last cat suffered from this and I did not find that having the teeth scaled was helpful for long. Yindee is a very active and fit kitten. I occasionally give her skirt [lower flank, usually of beef] but could you please advise any other way I could help prevent gingivitis developing?

P.P., Neath

Older cats will often not tolerate having their teeth brushed, but Yindee is young enough to learn. Get some meat-flavoured toothpaste from your vet or pet shop, and put it on your finger. "Sit with the cat between your knees facing away from you," says Evelyn Barbour-Hill, a vet with a special interest in dentistry. "Then push your finger under her lips from the front to the back of her cheek. Maybe she will only allow one side to be done at first, but don't attempt to force her or make her struggle. Even this much cleaning helps. When a cat is used to the finger, you can try a toothbrush, a soft cat one. Daily brushing is valuable even if it is a bit haphazard. You don't have to brush up and down; sweep sideways.'' There is also a special diet for cats prone to gingivitis available from vets. Some vets also sell special fishy cat chews, which help keep teeth clean.

Odd Tastes

My ten-year-old Siamese cross, Bella, has suddenly taken to fish-sticks, the light, floating variety. She goes raving mad while I am feeding and talking to the fish, so she has to have her share! Are they doing her any harm?

N.F., Devizes, Wiltshire

These sticks contain fishmeal, so they are tasty for cats as well as fish. As long as they are the packed kind sold by a reputable commercial firm, their contents will be edible for cats as well as fish. But only give her the occasional nibble. They are not a balanced diet.

Burbage our blue Burmese and several other cats I know, all go potty over home-made mince pies. True ecstasy is found in Delia Smith's fruit cake made with mincemeat. Indeed, mincemeat seems irresistible to cats. We used to leave a packet of "Fruit and Fibre" cereal out on the dining table ready for breakfast until we came downstairs one morning to find the packet contents strewn all over the floor – with the raisins all missing. At Christmas Burbage likes the cake but he's not wild about icing sugar or marzipan and he spits out the glacé cherries.

D.H-S., Dulwich

Burbage is only one of the many cats with extraordinary tastes ranging from raisins to Radio malt extract. Some of their favourites are predictable milky ones like expensive ice cream, rice pudding, Avocaat, puffed wheat with milk, and all kinds of cheese including Stilton. But these supposedly carnivore cats also like cake, Ryvita biscuits, cake icing, rice, crisps, raw pastry, toast, scones, and wallpaper paste. Cats are supposed not to taste sweetness, yet some Telegraph *cats adore Galaxy chocolate, marshmallows, Munchies, and the sugar on shortbread and toffees. One* Telegraph *cat used to take the wrapper off a toffee before chewing it.*

Odder is the range of fruit and vegetables they will eat — asparagus, mushrooms, raw runner beans, cauliflower, beetroot, cabbage, corn on the cob husks, melon, red pepper, spinach, broccoli, stewed plums with custard (perhaps this is the custard), banana sandwiches, green and black olives. There are also cats who enjoy curry, chilli con carne, fish food pellets, orange squash, fresh coffee, and "mango and chapattis".

But why, if cats are carnivores, do they eat doughnuts, cake and even vegetables? "Cats have something called the organ of Jacobson, which allows them to smell and analyze exactly what amino acids are in food," explains John Foster, a vet with a special interest in nutrition. "So in all these unlikely foods, there must be an amino acid which they want. They are carnivores not just because they eat meat, but because they have to eat forty-three different amino acids, and nothing else will do."

John Foster warns us, however, not to let our cats eat too much of these odd foods. "Cats are poor at digesting starches and while the odd raisin does no harm, large amounts of Christmas cake will not be good for them." Chocolate in large quantities is poisonous for both cats and dogs.

Feline Drinking Habits

Our cat, Perdy, has a peculiar attitude to water. She won't drink it from her bowl but, as soon as a tap is turned on, she jumps into the sink and gulps the running water. She loves water, but only when it's moving. She has thick fur and a long bushy tail and we are certain she is of mixed breed. Is there a type of cat that is known to behave in this way?

N.S., South-west London

Perhaps your cat has some Turkish van cat blood in its ancestry. Turkish vans sometimes actually swim. Another possibility is some Maine coon ancestry. Maine coons are known to spend a lot of time sitting under the tap, either in hope of a mouse popping out or because they are interested in water.

The other possibility is that Perdy drinks from the tap because it smells better. Cats hate the chemicals which are put in drinking water to make it safe to drink. When they drink from a bowl, they have time to sniff the chemicals first. When the water comes out of a tap, it may be that there isn't time for them to get a whiff of chemicals.

My son has a tabby cat, called Sam, who has very thick hair and a long bushy tail. He loves to drink from a running tap and jumps into washbasins, sinks, and the bath when available. He is a Maine coon. I thought your owner of Perdy might be interested.

M.R., Salisbury

My son's cat, Herbie, also prefers to drink from the tap despite having a small bowl on his eating mat in the kitchen. This habit has finally been broken by providing a larger water bowl, to accommodate his whiskers. According to my son, cats gauge size by the width of their whiskers and his bowl was just too small.

G.M., Cambridge

We have a leaky radiator in the kitchen and keep a margarine tub underneath to catch the drips. Can you explain why our cat, Chip (a perfectly ordinary tabby) keeps trying to drink the water out of the tub? He always has access to a bowl of water, but he seems to prefer the radiator water.

P.G., High Peak, Derbyshire

Outdoor Drinker

Our three-year-old tortoiseshell cat, Benson, has suddenly acquired a taste for the water in the bird bath and refuses all tap water. Will it do him harm?

D.H., Bridgwater, Somerset

Cats dislike the chemicals in tap water. They prefer even the filthiest puddle water or, according to one reader, water in which she has soaked her dirty hankies! It doesn't seem to do them any harm! I have started giving my cats water from a rainwater butt or even still mineral water, in an attempt to wean them off dirty puddles. They prefer it to tap water, but still enjoy a dirty puddle! Readers who want to keep cats from drinking from a goldfish pond can make a boggy area all round the pond. Cats don't like getting their feet wet.

Due South Drinker

My eleven-year-old British blue cat Mickey (definitely not named after Mickey Mouse) hates fish and never climbs trees. I assume this is because his ancestors lived in a treeless fishless desert. Whenever he drinks water (he is no lover of milk) he moves round so that he faces due south. Are my assumptions correct and are these peculiarities common to all British blues or other related breeds?

J.Y., North-west London

Till this letter arrived, I had heard of many cats who won't eat fish, some who won't climb trees, but never one (of any breed) that only drinks water when facing due south. I thought Mickey must be making a feline joke aimed at his owners but several readers wrote in to tell me that their cats insisted on the same alignment to their water bowl!

Messy Manners

We once had a particularly lofty cat who always wanted his food bowl to be placed in a certain position on a strip of carpet in the kitchen. If ever the meal proved not to his liking, he would pick up one end of this carpet by the claws of one front paw, and drag it across his plate until the offending offering was completely covered, then walk over it to go out. There was no question of his coming back later to "unbury" the food. After all *he* had condemned it as unfit for feline consumption. I should add that the degree of contempt radiated during these performances guaranteed that something different appeared on the menu when he returned.

D.C., Pwllheli, Gwynedd

Some of the large wild cats store half-eaten prey up trees, so they can come back and eat it later. "When they paw round the food bowl, cats seem to be burying the food remains," says Ian Robinson, behaviourist and vet. "You will see a cat eating a bit then going through the motions in the air. Then they will come back and eat the food." But some cats do this with food they do not like very much. Thus the cat may either be hiding away food with a view to finishing it off later, or it may be clearing up its territory by "burying" food it no long wants.

Picking up Food

Although I try to dissuade her, Blackie my five-year-old female cat will insist on picking up pieces of her tinned food and taking it from the kitchen into the lounge, which is an adjacent room, where she eats it. As you can imagine my carpet is suffering. Please can you help?

G.B., Thorpe Bay, Essex

Cats tend to take their food to somewhere where they feel secure, before eating it. Blackie may be moving the food because to her the sitting room feels safer than the kitchen. Is the food bowl in the kitchen near dogs, other cats, people's feet or children? Or perhaps the kitchen is not as comfortable as the sitting room – uncarpeted, draughty or colder.

See if you can find a better arrangement for the bowl in the kitchen. And you could just shut the sitting-room door, if there is one. It is difficult to persuade cats to change their habits, so maybe you will have to give Blackie dry food (with water nearby) which will be less messy.

Compulsive Chewer

My five-year-old Tonkinese, William, started to chew the corners of newspapers while eating his meal. He has now moved on to telephone wires and his wicker bed. We give him a cardboard box every week that he chews and chews. This can't be good for him but we don't know how to stop him. We have taken him to the vet who checked his teeth and says there is no dental reason for his behaviour.

C.W., Ilminster, Somerset

Cats would normally be crunching up mice whole, fur and bones included. But with tinned food they are getting none of this roughage. "Nutritionally, tinned food provides an excellent diet but the cat feels hungry so it starts chewing," says Peter Neville, pet behaviour counsellor. Chewing becomes a rewarding experience in itself. "Give him a more diverse diet, including dry food and gristly meat. Better still, give the meat still attached to a leg bone so that he really has to chew at it." Other chewy things might include the wing tips (not the rest of the wing) of raw (never cooked) chicken and the gristly part of the breastbone (not the bony part). Also chunks of ox heart or pig heart – so that the cat has to chew at them.

Leaving dry food down will help direct his chewing at food not wires, but keep an eye on his weight."

Peter Neville suggests buying little bangers from joke shops. "These are pressure sensitive. Arrange them so they go bang when the cat chews a wire." This might be too much for an old or nervous cat, however. If the behaviour continues, ask your vet to refer you to a pet behaviour counsellor as this habit is potentially dangerous.

Cure for Crunching

I was recommended a cure for cats who try to chew electric cables. That is, paint the cable with Tabasco. It proved most effective. Our cat objected to the household looking at television when he felt it detracted from his being noticed. He would walk behind the TV set and take the lead in his mouth and stare at everyone. Obviously the response was what he wanted: everyone leapt up to stop him actually biting it. The effect of the Tabasco lasted for a few days, when a new application was needed. I put some Tabasco in an old nail varnish bottle as it had a brush and was easy to administer. This tip may be of interest to cat owners who have similar problems.

E.T., Richmond, Surrey

This is a good idea for most cats. Those sophisticated cats who enjoy a curry, however, may simply chew all the more!

Cats who Love too Much, Cats who Don't Love at All, Neurotic Cats and Cats who Think Their Head is a Mouse

Just as the child is father to the man, so the kitten is father to the adult cat. A happy kittenhood, with lots of human contact, will produce a loving pet cat. A dysfunctional kittenhood, without proper human contact, will usually mean a neurotic cat that never fully trusts human beings.

There is what experts call a "sensitive period" from two to seven weeks, during which a kitten must be handled by human beings in order to become a domestic pet. Kittens that miss out on this period will always have difficulties relating to humans. Some cats seem to get on better with women than with men, probably because during kittenhood they were handled by women rather than men. In the same way, a kitten must meet friendly dogs during this period, if it is to be friendly with dogs as an adult. This is why it is so important to choose a kitten who has had a proper upbringing in the first weeks of its life. Never buy a pedigree kitten from a breeder whose kittens are kept in a cat chalet rather than the kitchen. Never buy a kitten from a pet shop, as only unscrupulous breeders sell to such shops.

Many of the problem cats whose owners write to me have probably had a dysfunctional kittenhood. In later life, therefore, these cats are frightened personalities, unhappy with cuddling, sometimes lashing out with teeth or claw from fear. With patience, they can be tamed somewhat but will probably never change into really placid cats. They exhibit what experts call the "petting and biting syndrome", when the cat responds to petting with aggression. They may seek out human affection and appear for a few moments to enjoy petting, then turn on the petter with either teeth or claws.

Other cats, usually rescue cats, seem wild because of a traumatic experience in their life. Many stray cats meet with abuse or downright cruelty from human beings while they are living rough. These cats, though at first they seem completely wild, will usually learn to trust again and the snarling spitting savage will become the quiet cat purring on its owner's lap.

Occasionally an otherwise docile cat will attack because it is aroused by something else. For instance, if it is watching another cat through the window, it may turn on its owner. It is always worth checking to see if there is some new threat in the cat's life – a new neighbouring cat, for instance. A cat in pain – from a hidden abscess perhaps – may also bite, so rule out such possibilities by visiting the vet.

At the other end of the spectrum are the Cats Who Love Too Much. These too have had a dysfunctional kittenhood of a different kind. Many of them have been bottle-reared by human beings or taken too young from their mothers. Sometimes their emotional neediness is the result of a long period of illness during which they were completely reliant on humans. (Such an experience, incidentally, can occasionally change a hitherto wild cat into one happy to be handled by humans.) This need is often expressed by kittenish behaviour – sucking at human skin or clothing, kneading, or following their owners around, mewing. Such behaviour can be quite flattering for human beings, who may unthinkingly encourage it by, for instance, responding with even more love and tenderness. These cats need gentle encouragement to be more independent.

Emotionally needy cats sometimes turn into

chronic attention seekers, as do bored cats with not enough to do during the day. Oriental breeds, who are usually more vocal than moggies, can become positive tyrants, demanding attention by almost constant yowling. But even well-balanced cats can develop irritating behaviour in order to get human attention. Watch your cat as he scratches the furniture, for instance, or pushes something off the mantelpiece. You may see him looking at you for your reaction whether it is laughing, picking him up or even shouting. Verbal abuse, after all, is attention.

We humans have to learn new tricks in return. We must respond to attention-seeking behaviour by withdrawing our attention. We can walk out of the room, or turn our whole body, including eyes and face, away and start paying attention to something else. Attention-seeking behaviour should die out when it is no longer rewarded by our attention.

In addition we must give the attention-seeking cat lots of attention when he is doing something we want him to do, like sitting on our lap, or purring quietly. Reward him with attention for keeping quiet, or teach him something else to do to attract our attention. A nice little trick like begging might be the answer!

Not all cats can be retrained successfully into new habits. Researchers have proved that a cat can inherit its temperament from its parents. Thus, aloof cats have kittens which will also grow up to be aloof.

Finally, some cats suffer from stereotypic behaviour, a compulsive habit which apparently serves no useful purpose in the animal's life. There is a stereotypic behaviour among Burmese cats in which the animals attack their own faces. Some will pull the skin and fur off the whole of the side of their face. As this has so far only been found in the one breed, it may be some kind of inherited disorder.

Tail-biting is a severe form of stereotypic disorder. The cat somehow gets "hooked" on the pain and repeatedly mutilates itself. This may be the animal's response to some upsetting earlier experience, an attempt to avoid pain or discomfort, or some kind of brain damage. I have included three letters on the subject, all with different outcomes.

Severe behaviour disorders like these are very difficult indeed to cure permanently. Jacob, a tail-biting cat from one of the following letters, had seen his vet, an animal psychologist, and a veterinary neurologist before his owners wrote to me. He had had his teeth examined, his whole body X-rayed, and tried all kinds of drugs. When Jacob was finally put down, his owner wrote to me explaining, "We just couldn't bear to see him suffer any longer. He began to have fits of tail chasing and self-injury two, three and sometimes more times a day. We feared for him and finally decided that it would be better and kinder for him to be put down."

Such cats give us the chance to show the fullest expression of human love. Jacob's owners make me feel more hopeful about the human race.

Dashing and Biting

Tufty, my neutered former stray cat, dashes from bushes and chairs and sinks his teeth and claws into my legs which can be painful and bloody. Even the paper boy and postman have only stroked him once and never again. He can be sitting on my lap, but as soon as I stroke him, his teeth are very much in evidence. I have tried kindness, a rolled-up newspaper, gentle spanks on the rear. A neighbour suggested he was a feral cat, but I have had him nine years. My husband, not a cat lover, says have him put down.

D.M. Hertford

Tufty was probably wrongly brought up. Kittens need human contact in the first ten weeks, if they are to be properly domesticated, and perhaps he didn't have this. "There is no point at all in punishing him, not even with a rolled-up newspaper," says Dr David Sands, a pet behaviour counsellor. "Try clapping your hands loudly, as he launches himself, but don't shout," he advises. The idea is to distract him at the crucial moment. "You could also throw a squeaky toy or a mouse treated with catnip in front of him, to divert him away from your legs."

Dr Sands also wonders if Tufty needs more interesting toys and scratching posts. "More play and exploration time might use up his natural tendency to have wild periods." Older cats also sometimes need their diet reviewed, in case high protein is triggering wild behaviour, so ask your vet about this.

Frankly, it is easier to change dog behaviour than cat behaviour. Some cats just aren't cuddly, particularly if they had a feral kittenhood. "You just have to respect that cat's position," says Dr Sands.

Petting and Biting

Gus, our eighteen-month-old neutered tomcat, can choose what to do with his time via his cat flap and we live in a place with very good hunting. He is very affectionate, loves to be picked up for a cuddle or to settle on a lap, but within a very short time he starts to bite and scratch very nastily. Is this just rough sibling play that he will grow out of? Or is there something we can do about it?

M.E., Foyers, Inverness-shire

Kittens need human handling between the ages of two and seven weeks to feel comfortable with petting. Perhaps Gus was deprived of the right kind of handling in kittenhood, so he is now the victim of what experts call the "petting and biting syndrome". You can help him with patient reha-bilitation sessions!

"When Gus has settled on your lap, stroke the least sensitive parts of his body, such as the back and head. Avoid sensitive areas like the tummy," says Sarah Heath, vet and pet behaviour counsellor. "Keep these petting sessions short, and always end them before he reacts with biting. Give him the chance to get away when he feels like it and never restrain him."

If you gradually increase the length of these sessions, but always stop them before he flips into attack mode, you will help Gus learn to tolerate petting. "This Jekyll and Hyde behaviour can be upsetting," says Sarah Heath, "but it's quite common, and many owners have scratched hands to prove it."

Controlling and Biting

We have a rescue cat, Pompey, a tabby of about four years old. He is affectionate, and will sit on our laps, but I am sure he has been ill-treated, as he has now bitten me three times. Perhaps this is why he was rejected in the first place. We will be getting on fine, but if I move him, or haven't the time to play, he reaches out with claws outstretched, meows at me, and then will bite if he can reach. It's surely a bullying way of holding my attention and affection. It is my hand he bites, and on the second occasion I had to have penicillin as the wound became infected. My husband says he should go. Do you have any suggestions?

E.M., Lingfield, Surrey

Pompey may be trying to keep control of the situation, stopping you moving him when he doesn't want to be moved, or getting your attention when he wants it. You have to show him that you, not he, call the shots. "First of all, you need to find a way of moving him without getting bitten," says Daniel Mills, a vet who runs an animal behaviour clinic. "You could use oven mitts, or entice him out of the way with a fishing-rod toy, or push him with a piece of wood covered with soft fabric."

Schedule times to play with him or pet him, starting and stopping when you, not he, choose. At times when he bites or claws you, make a sharp hissing noise at him, the feline way of saying "Naff off". "This will interrupt his behaviour and he will retreat," explains Daniel Mills. "Next, you call him to you again with a treat and interact with him. Then you stop the game and walk away." If you keep doing this, he should begin to see that you are the one to start and stop petting and play.

You should also look for signs that he is getting aroused, which could lead to an attack, and stop the game or petting session before the attack takes place. You may then be able to get him used to a steadily greater amount of handling. The secret is not to push him too far too soon.

Nervous Jasper

Jasper, our rescue tabby, runs outside to some unknown haven during heavy rain or thunderstorms. As soon as the rain starts, he is agitated and spurns all our attempts to make him feel at ease. He was found as a stray when three months old. As doting owners it has proved rather disconcerting to find that for him our home is not a haven. Can you throw some light on his behaviour?

D.P., King's Lynn, Norfolk

Both cats and dogs can become terrified of thunder. It's difficult enough to reduce dogs' fears and I think it would be impossible, at the moment, to change how Jasper feels. If he was once a stray, Jasper may have been brought up out of doors from kittenhood. If so, he instinctively dashes for home when he's scared and so far, for him, a house is not a home. It may take months, even years, before he thinks of indoors as his safest refuge. In the meantime why not shut the cat flap at night? It's during the dark hours that Jasper is most likely to get run over as he rushes for cover. Your chances of finding where he goes are slim.

Cats Who Love Too Much

Alice, my young cat, was reared on a bottle. She has a funny habit of climbing up on my chest and "making bread". She puts her head in my armpit and sucks flesh or wool. Should I try to stop this habit?

D.S., Ipplepen, Devon

Usually it is humans who love cats too much, but this is, potentially at least, a Cat Who Loves Too Much. Cats reared by humans sometimes become overdependent on them, *according to Sarah Heath, a vet and cat behaviour counsellor. The overdependent cat may knead and suck either flesh or clothing, may cry at night, and make excessive demands for physical contact. Just occasionally this develops into spraying in the house, hiding in dark corners if the owners are out, over-grooming, self-mutilation, or wool eating. "The bond must be decreased and the basis of the relationship between owner and cat needs to be altered," advises Sarah Heath. A good feline mother gently pushes away growing kittens who knead and suck too long. You should do the same to Alice, making sure that any rejection is of a non-punishing nature. In general encourage Alice to be more independent.*

Emotionally Needy Daisy

I have two Burmese, Freda and Daisy. When I go away for a night, Daisy starts licking herself, and pulling at her fur. Daisy is very clinging. She follows me from room to room, and when she goes out comes back to check that I am still there. She will run after me mewing and, when I am watching TV, within ten minutes she is on my lap or touching my body. Freda has more confidence. Daisy was once locked in the wardrobe for six hours, when I was away. The fur pulling started after that.

J.L., South-east London

This looks like separation anxiety, which is common in dogs. "But it can't happen with cats as they are not strictly speaking social animals. Daisy has got over-attached and the running after her owner mewing is kitten behaviour," says Emma Magnus, a pet behaviour counsellor. She suggests weakening what is rather too intense a relationship. To do this, Daisy's emotionally needy behaviour must not be rewarded by your attention. "If Daisy is in need of affection, be aloof," says Emma Magnus. "Give her plenty of affection, but only when she is not demanding it so you are rewarding her for not being demanding. Also do not feed on demand, but feed at set times."

Dribbling

Can anything be done about a cat which is a copious dribbler? Bibbity really loves to be cuddled but anyone who co-operates in this is instantly saturated. He only dribbles with pleasure and satisfaction at loving attention, not in any other circumstances.

H.T., Redhill, Surrey

You will have just to love him, dribbles and all. "But if a cat suddenly starts to dribble, when not being cuddled, it may be a sign of dental pain, difficulty swallowing, mouth irritation or even brain disease," warns David Godfrey, a vet from a veterinary practice which specializes in cats. In this case, see a vet promptly.

Licking

Our male cat, Jess, whom we adopted two years ago, has always had a strange habit of licking. He will frantically lick our hands, legs, arms and also his toys. He doesn't lick himself bald. Why is he doing this?

H.J., Chingford, East London

"It's kitten behaviour," explains Peter Neville, a cat behaviour counsellor. "They would suck, only there is no milk. So licking is the next best thing to sucking. If you want to stop it, get up and walk away the second that Jess starts doing it. He will then find something else to give him that feeling of closeness."

Emotionally Demanding Burt

We have two black moggies, Daisy and Burt, who are brother and sister. Daisy comes for cuddles when she wants and behaves as a cat should. However, Burt requires constant human contact. As we work from home, and have computers, phones etc., it is really very difficult. We have to push him off twenty to thirty times a day, but we always make sure that he gets plenty of petting as well. He does not fully retract his claws and really hurts as he paddles, so we have padded mats for our laps when we relax during the evening. I have to admit I am beginning to dread the sight of him approaching, yet I am afraid he will decide to move on to find a home where he can be doted on twenty-four hours a day. Please, any ideas?

V.M., Huddersfield, West Yorkshire

Burt is clearly another Cat Who Loves Too Much! At the moment you are rejecting him when you don't want him on your lap, but petting him when you do. "This is a schedule of occasional reward, which is more rewarding than a schedule of constant reward," says Peter Neville, a cat behaviour counsellor. "Burt is frustrated when he is pushed off, so tries harder, and when he is rewarded by petting, he gets not just the reward but relief from the frustration."

Peter Neville suggests introducing a signal for the times when you do not want him to jump up. It must be a sound not heard at other times like a whistle or a little bell. Both you and your husband must use the same sound. "Use the signal just before he lands on your lap. If he does land, then get up and walk away without using your hands to push him off."

You can also introduce a signal for the times when it is all right for him to be on your lap. This signal could just be putting the padded mats on your lap, or it could be a different sound. It's going to be hard work putting this into practice at the beginning. "You both have to be completely consistent about this, otherwise it won't work," warns Peter Neville. "It will probably take at least two weeks."

Cat Behaving Badly

It was love at first sight when Tipsy-Topsy-Boy arrived as a little kitten but now he is wrecking my life! His favourite game is pushing every object off tables and mantelpieces. I have now got to the stage when I think something must be wrong if things don't drop on my head at 3 a.m. Everything breakable in my flat has to remain at ground level. At night he gets into bed and suckles my left earlobe. I take him to see my mother and he tries continually to mount her cat, Suki. He goes berserk after food and charges around in a frenzy.

C.M., West London

This is only part of a much longer letter about Tipsy-Topsy-Boy who has his owner firmly under his paw and is a Cat Behaving Badly, determined to get his owner's attention at all times! "The bond between owner and cat needs to be loosened," says Emma Magnus, a pet behaviour counsellor. "Tipsy-Topsy needs to be rewarded when he is quiet and ignored when he is attention seeking." Do not feed him on demand, but feed at set times. Remain aloof when he demands affection; instead, give it to him when he is not being demanding.

To stop him waking you at 3 a.m., you could simply shut him out of the bedroom at night. "If you don't want to do this, then you can simply ignore him altogether by getting under the duvet. When he doesn't get the attention after several nights he will stop doing it. If this is too difficult, each time he wakes you up in this way, walk with him outside the room and shut him out." During the daytime, you can try to deny him access to the mantelpiece by diverting his attention with a toy or game.

You may, without realizing it, be encouraging him to pester your mother's cat by giving him attention when he does this. Even shouting or rebuking him is attention. Just ignore this behaviour. Young cats often pester adults with pouncing or mounting, but adult cats are usually quite good at telling them where to get off.

Begging Tabby

Can you offer an explanation as to why Suki, our long-haired silver tabby, aged one year, has taken to sitting on her back legs and pawing the air for periods of up to one minute? Naturally this behaviour amuses us. She does not appear to be begging for food and she is in every other way an ordinary happy cat.

P.M., Harrow, Middlesex

Pets, like young children, love getting their owners' attention. Suki is succeeding! "The first time she did this was perhaps almost by accident, but your reaction was such that she quickly learned it was a way of getting you to notice her," says Sarah Heath, vet and pet behaviour counsellor. "The other possibility, which seems less likely since Suki is a well-balanced cat, is that this is stereotypic behaviour." Some cats develop stereotypic habits like this, which can be quite severe, and in these cases they need treatment from a pet behaviour counsellor.

Stereotypic

My eleven-year-old cat, Bella, has recently developed the most odd behaviour. She will take a couple of paces, stop and stare intently at the ground as if watching an insect, take another two paces, stop and stare – over and over again. Even odder, her mother, Lily, who lives with my daughter has been doing the same thing for the past few months. Any explanations?

M.D., Bridport, Dorset

Cats are hunters, and so have an instinctive need to look for prey, stalk it, chase it, pounce on and kill it. "Bella's behaviour is stuck at the beginning of this hunting sequence," says Peter Neville, cat behaviour counsellor. "She is staring, stalking and then repeating it rather than advancing through the whole sequence." If this was a young cat, she might just need to be taught the proper sequence. You could do this by using dangling toys to encourage her to chase and pounce. Once she had learned the proper sequence, she should be able to perform it.

"Since this is an old cat, it may be possible that this is some kind of temporal lobe disturbance," says Peter Neville. "Something triggers the initial stare and stalk, then comes mild seizure activity, not severe enough to cause a fit. This makes Bella go blank and she simply starts again." The fact that Bella's mother Lily is showing the same behaviour suggests there may be some inherited disorder. "There's no way of testing, except to ask the vet to give Bella a very tiny dose of anti-epilepsy drugs. If she gets better, then it probably was a temporal lobe disorder." Getting treatment is only necessary if you think Bella's behaviour might prove dangerous for her when she needs to react fast, e.g. when faced with an angry dog or traffic on the road.

Burmese Self-mutilation

When he was eight months old, my neutered male Burmese cat started to claw at his teeth and gums until he bled. Sometimes he would extend his tongue as if retching or in pain at the back of his throat. A vet's examination of mouth and throat revealed nothing. The symptoms disappeared for seven years but have returned with a vengeance. Fred pulled the skin and fur off one side of his face before I could get him to the vet. Teeth were extracted, examinations were carried out, and he was put under deep sedation, but the behaviour is continuing. Can you shed any light on this?

S.S., Taplow, Berkshire

This mysterious behaviour seems to occur only in Burmese and may be an inherited disorder. Several cases have been seen by vet Robin Walker and cat behaviour counsellor Peter Neville. They believe it is misdirected and obsessive predatory behaviour. "It is as if the cat thinks its head is a mouse," says Walker. He suggests keeping handy some Valium, prescribed by a vet, to give to Fred at the first sign of an episode to calm him down.

Neville suggests putting Fred on an all-chicken diet.

"Among those we have treated two seem to have been cured by this, but it will take three weeks for any change to be noticed," he says. *"Those we have seen have been indoor cats, so it is worth trying to make sure their predatory needs are fulfilled."* Cats in the wild will make roughly thirty pounces a day (successful and unsuccessful) on their prey. If Fred is an indoor cat, play games with him with fishing-rod toys, pieces of string, or feathers tied to a little rod.

Tail Mutilation

Jacob, our cat whom we rescued from a cruel home, has "turns" when he bites his own tail. It starts during a self-grooming session. He glares at the tip of his tail, catches it, and bites right into the bone. Then he screams in pain and runs. If we are near to him when he starts, we can stop the cycle by clapping our hands or shouting. He has seen a psychologist, and a neurologist, and is currently on Valium. If we forget to give him a pill, it is likely to happen. Do you have any suggestions as to how we can improve his quality of life?

P.R., Scarborough, North Yorkshire

Tail biting is a severe form of stereotypic behaviour. The animal (more often a dog) somehow gets "hooked" on the pain and repeatedly mutilates itself. Jacob was rescued from a cruel owner, and his compulsion may have developed during his unhappy early life.

"It is rare in cats, and we don't know much about the cause," says Vicky Halls, a cat behaviour counsellor. *"Just training Jacob out of this compulsive behaviour would be very difficult indeed. I think that Jacob's owners are doing the right thing in trying to interrupt the cycle, but to have any long-term success they would have to do this every single time.*

"In America they are experimenting with human anti-obsessional drugs for this kind of behaviour, which they have called feline hyperaesthetic syndrome. If Jacob's owners are not happy about the Valium, it would be worth discussing this possibility with their vet."

Weeny was the runt of the litter, and developed an irregular muscle spasm in her back leg. When the spasm shot through her, she would whirl round and sink her teeth into the nearest thing, which was her tail. The tail was cut off by the vet as it became infected. Now she has a scut instead of a tail, and the leg spasms are quite rare.

P.B., North London

Mac is an indoor cat and has had two episodes of tail biting. Fearful that this was caused by the stress of boredom (I am out all day), I improved his environment by adding a tall cat aerobic system and tried to give him more play time. However, on the second episode, the vet discovered dental disease on one tooth. She thinks that tooth pain may have caused him to bite his tail.

J.M., South London

Sex, Hatred, Sibling Rivalry and Kitten Abuse

Cats can and do live happily together. There is no pack hierarchy among them (with the occasional exception of some oriental breeds) but nor are they necessarily solitary animals. They are happy in a community if there is plenty of food and space. If not, then they spread out on their own into a larger hunting territory.

The house is usually a cat's core territory and several cats, if they are introduced correctly and have been spayed and neutered, can live together in harmony. However, the greater the number of cats in a house, the greater the likelihood of squabbles, rivalry, bullying and occasionally settled hatred. Genuine hatred on both sides is difficult to change, which makes it important to intervene as soon as possible if things are going wrong.

Cats sometimes have a relationship which is remote but not abusive. They may live in different parts of the house, or in different rooms, with separate litter trays. If this is an acceptable relationship to them, and neither cat seems to be suffering, then it should be acceptable to you, the owner.

It is always worth taking care, when introducing a new cat or kitten to the household. The initial reaction of the existing cats is almost always hostile. Far from welcoming a new playfellow or mothering a sweet little kitten, they treat the incomer with disdain and even downright anger.

It is important to distinguish between normal squabbles and real warfare. Chasing games and the occasional tiff with hissing, puffed-up fur and paw slapping can exist within a reasonable relationship. If, however, these are accompanied by bites or real scratches, then the relationship has seriously broken down. This can happen if something – a visit to the vet perhaps – changes the smell of a previously accepted cat. When the cat returns home it smells like and is therefore treated as an intruder. A fight breaks out and the cats become more wary of each other, making a second fight more likely – just like partners in a bad human marriage! Similarly, if two cats from the same family are housed separately in a cattery, then they may go back to treating each other as strangers when they return home.

Feline pregnancy within the home may also produce stress and aggression. When a cat is pregnant or nursing kittens, she will attack others. Sometimes when the pregnancy is over, things settle down. Alternatively, when the kittens are grown up, mothers and the new adults may not be able to exist in harmony. A new cat introduced into the household can also change group dynamics.

Occasionally, the problem is an intruding cat who comes in through the cat flap. Stray cats, and even well-fed pet cats, get very clever at sneaking into the house and eating other felines' food. This is bound to upset the incumbent cats. There may be fights or the resident cats may simply disappear in terror under the beds. A neighbouring cat bully can make your own cats' lives miserable. They will come home with cuts and bites, or the abscesses that arise from untreated bites, making all-over body checks a daily necessity. Sometimes they will just refuse to go out at all, unless they are bodyguarded by you.

Cats can also become stressed and anxious if a dog is coming into their garden, or even, in the case of small dogs, through the cat flap. Visiting foxes and badgers may also make them feel very uneasy. Even changes in the household or household routine can affect their feeling of security. A new baby, a new boyfriend, or builders working in the house – even new furniture – can induce anxiety. They may start scent-marking their territory to make themselves feel more secure, which usually means the incredibly smelly habit of spraying. This is not normal urination, when the cat squats. To spray, a cat stands upright with tail quivering and a jet of urine marks what is usually a vertical object, like a tree, an armchair, a door or a piece of furniture.

Un-neutered tomcats almost always spray their territory anyway, which is why they are unsuitable as domestic pets. But ordinary neutered males and spayed females will also spray when they feel worried. Any kind of punishment will make them feel even more anxious, and they will spray even more, to mark their territory and reassure themselves that the territory belongs to them. Once an area has been sprayed, the cat will respray it as the scent begins to fade. So it is important to deal with spraying as soon as possible.

Till recently, the only hope of persuading a cat not to respray a sprayed surface was very careful cleaning. Using biological washing liquid, the whole surface had to be cleaned, then scrubbed with surgical spirit. To make the area unattractive for spraying, beds and feeding bowls had to be moved as near as possible to the sprayed surface. Cats do not spray where they eat or sleep. At the same time, to make it feel safe in its own territory, the cat could be put in a small room or in an indoor pen with its own bed and litter tray. Then, by slowly allowing it access to the house room by room over several days, the hope was that the moggie would slowly perceive the whole house as a safe zone.

Nowadays there is a new chemical devised to mimic cats' own scentmarking. Cats not only scentmark by spraying; they also scentmark by chin rubbing. Where they rub, they do not spray. So vets now stock an aerosol which, to a cat, smells like a chin-rubbing scent. This, if it is used lavishly and repeatedly, will often put a stop to respraying.

The fundamental reasons for a cat's anxiety, however, still need to be discovered, then treated. To diagnose them you can try various experiments. Install an electronic cat flap to repel intruders, or close the cat flap altogether to give a greater feeling of safety. Also, either cover or block access to windows or glass doors that give a view of the garden, where a threatening animal may be causing the anxiety.

Finding the reason why cats are feeling stressed is often difficult for the owner, who is too close to the problem to see it clearly. Consulting a good cat behaviour counsellor is expensive but, like seeing a marriage guidance counsellor, it may produce a more satisfactory solution than rehoming an otherwise recalcitrant cat.

Merging Families and Pets

I have two dogs – Jess, a border collie, and Digger, a Labrador – and one cat, Sammy. My fiancée has two young cats, Socks and Jarvis. Soon we will marry and merge our two animal families. We will be moving to a new property. Do you have any advice to help the transition?

G.H., Canterbury, Kent

Luckily Jess and Digger are already used to cats. You can get your fiancée's cats acquainted with them before moving by taking one dog at a time – two together sometimes egg each other on to chase – to visit Socks and Jarvis. "At first let the dog wander round a room without the cats, so that later when the cats return they can smell that the dog has been there," says pet behaviour counsellor, Erica Peachey. "After two or three visits, keep the dog on a lead, and let Socks and Jarvis feel free to wander in. They must also be free to leave – cats panic more if they feel they can't. Make sure there are high places for them to retreat to. Reward the dog with titbits for being calm."

Moving into a new house means that all the cats must be kept indoors for about a month. Start with the cats in separate rooms so that they get used to the new place. "If possible let them see each other through baby gates or perhaps an indoor crate – though this can frighten some cats. After a little while let the cats eat their meals in the same room, at first at different ends."

Keep the dogs away from the cats for at least two weeks and make sure the dogs are on a lead when they are introduced to the cats. If you hurry the introductions, things can go wrong. Patience is a must. "If this doesn't go smoothly, a great deal more can be done on an individual basis, with a programme tailor-made for each animal," says Erica Peachey.

Brotherly Rivalry

I have two Burmese castrated males, Jeremy who is one year old and Paxman who is two years old. They eat out of the same dish and sleep together on the bed. But after any attention is shown to Jeremy, Paxman will immediately go for him and chase him away.

G.J., Oxford

Are you sure this is really serious, not just rough-house playing and chasing? "If cats eat out of the same dish, they are usually reasonably good friends," says Sarah Heath, a vet and cat behaviour counsellor. "Normally, feeding cats in the same dish promotes harmony! The signs of serious hostility are hissing, growling, coat ruffled up, ears back and possibly biting. If this is going on, then you have a serious problem. Remove the trigger which in this case seems to be your attention. Stop giving them attention when both are in the same room and only pet them when they are apart."

Cats do not have a structured hierarchy like dogs but occasionally something like it is seen in Burmese and other oriental cats. *"It might help to make Paxman more secure, and demote Jeremy, the younger one,"* suggests Sarah Heath. This sounds like encouraging bullying, but the idea is to stop disagreements by making one cat unquestionably in charge! *"Sometimes two same-sex cats are so incompatible that you have to think about rehoming one."*

Hatred in the Home

We inherited my late mother-in-law's cat, Pru, six months ago. She had been an only cat but we already had three others. I am at my wit's end with all her spraying. And now because Pru − eleven years old at least − gets away with it (I never see her do it) Alice cat (nine years) thinks she can do it too. Alice and Pru loathe each other. Lizzie cat and TK cat hate her too.

D.B., Reading, Berkshire

Cats spray as a way of marking their territory, when they feel insecure. Both Pru and Alice feel this way. The easiest solution, which you will probably feel you can't do, would be to find Pru a new home where there are no feline competitors. However, it may be worth trying a new product, Feliway, which is based on the scent of cats' cheek pheromones.

"Cats rub their cheeks on areas to mark their territory," says Sarah Whitehead, a cat behaviour counsellor. *"The idea is that if areas are already marked with Feliway, cats won't need to spray urine on them. You need to spray Feliway on daily or twice daily for the first three weeks, then every other day."* For it to work properly, you will first have to scrub clean every single sprayed site using surgical spirit. Wait till this has completely dried before putting on the Feliway. *"It's also worth tripling the number of cat beds all over the house, and putting lots and lots of different bowls of cat food out,"* says Sarah

Whitehead. This way, there is less competition for beds and food.

If cats have been spraying for a long time, Feliway may only work if it is used lavishly daily over a very long period indeed. This can be so expensive that you may make the decision to rehome Pru instead.

Intruding Cat

Because of our alarm system our neutered cat, Alfie, has to be shut in the kitchen when we go out. There's a litter tray and a cat flap and he does not seem to spray any more. But we notice a strong smell when he has been alone there. A territorial dispute is raging with the local tom which has tried to come into the house occasionally but has been seen off. Our cat became stressed some weeks ago and had to have hormone treatment to stop hair loss from excessive washing. Is the smell some sort of scent given off by our cat in reaction to the tom?

M.T., Enfield, Middlesex

Assuming that you have checked for dead mice underneath the fridge, it may be that either he or his enemy is spraying while you are out. If so, you will find the sprayed areas on vertical surfaces about 20 cm above the floor. If poor Alfie has been grooming excessively, and you have ruled out the possibility of flea allergy, he may have been upset by this territorial dispute. You can help him feel secure by shutting the cat flap or installing a magnetic one which will keep out the tom. Also buy a water pistol and use it on the tom, when you get the chance.

"This may not be enough because Alfie may be able to see the tom from the kitchen," warns David Godfrey, a vet who specializes in cats. "So, if he is the one spraying, he may continue to do so. Ask your vet for Feliway, a product which mimics the scent of a cat's facial gland. The idea is to encourage Alfie to scentmark with his face, rather than with urine. Spray this on vertical surfaces where he has sprayed and also on the surfaces where you have seen him rub in the kitchen and in any other rooms which he uses a lot." If you

are using Feliway, don't clean the sprayed surfaces with biological washing powder first, because it may stop Feli-way working.

Family Breakdown

I have three British blue cats, all from the same breeder – a mother, Lily, and two female kittens, Helen and Penny. There is no cat flap. The cats are let in and out of my house through French windows opening out on to a first floor balcony. It was there the mother and her close daughter started to spray; the other daughter doesn't spray. Now they spray in the porch, under windows, and on the French windows to this balcony. All the places they spray potentially have a sight of the garden or are near a place where they can see the garden. A fox visits the garden at night and also a local cat (but not a bully). Now the whole house smells they are beginning to spray anywhere. The only place they don't spray is the kitchen and a utility room where they have their litter tray. So we confine them to this room. My husband says he can't take much more! What on earth can I do?

J.P., Rochester, Kent

Cats spray when they feel insecure and it may be that the presence of the fox and strange cat in the garden are the triggers for this behaviour. "Increasing security within the home with smaller but more frequent meals and with play sessions may help," advises Sarah Heath, cat behaviour counsellor. If you can cover up the bottom of the French windows so that the cats can't see out, this may also help them feel safe.

However, once cats have sprayed for whatever reason, the decaying scent will trigger them to respray. You can get your vet to prescribe Feliway, which smells of a cat's chin. Where cats rub their chins, they do not spray. "Cleaning up is the most important thing, but when using Feliway clean with water only and then surgical spirit. Do not use biological washing powder because it can break down the

Feliway, which needs to be applied every twenty-four hours. Use Feliway on the cats' usual walkways indoors, as well as the places previously soiled.''

Take the process slowly room by room, cleaning up and Feliwaying one room then letting the cats into it for a few days before starting on the next room. "In effect you are reintroducing the cats to their core territory and reassuring them that it is a secure place to be in," says Sarah Heath. "It is possible that tension between the cats within the household may be relevant in this case and this is something that could benefit from more investigation.''

Stopping Thuggish Behaviour

George, our half-Burmese panther-lookalike of eighteen-and-a-half years old, is an elderly reprobate. He has taken to getting into other houses, terrorizing poor little pussies and on occasion reducing them and their owners to the state of a jelly with his thuggish behaviour. Recently he got into a house where the cat flap was locked by ripping the door out. George was always a bruiser but this is getting out of hand. I value friendship with the people living here. Any suggestions?

C.L., Bridford, Devon

Buy several cheap long-range water pistols from a toy shop and present one to all the suffering neighbours. Suggest they load it with orange juice and keep it at the ready to aim at George. It won't seriously hurt him but it may make him less likely to break into other houses. It will also give them an outlet for their anger! If a neighbouring cat is *getting seriously upset, negotiate a time-share agreement whereby George is kept in for a certain time daily, while the other cat can get some exercise.*

For several years my two elderly lady cats, Minnie and Polly, have been on the receiving end of a feline thug who comes in through the cat flap, sprays the kitchen, eats their food and on one occasion was found fast asleep on our settee. I tried everything including using a water pistol but this can only be effective if one catches the offender in the act. My local Cats Protection League gave me a tip which so far (fingers crossed) has worked. A drop of oil of olbas, from a chemist's shop, put on the cat flap rim, or near the point of entry, has deterred our neighbourhood bully. Two or three drops applied at intervals through the day, and especially in the evening, seems to have done the trick without confusing my own cats.

A.G., Brentwood, Essex

Keeping out Intruders
Readers might like to know how we resolved the problem of keeping one cat, who is blind, indoors, and letting the other out.

First we installed an electronic cat flap. As the locking device only works in one direction, and is designed to prevent stray cats encroaching, we fitted it backwards. However, as the original point of entry/exit is through a cavity wall, this presented further problems in fitting and operation. I overcame these by building a perspex tunnel and fitting the electronic flap on one end but still retaining the original flap fitted to the wall. This meant that our cat had to negotiate two flaps but he soon got the hang of it.

Then we had further problems with a stray cat coming in, but being prevented from getting out.

This meant that the original standard cat flap fitted to the wall had to be replaced and the system would require yet another electronic flap to run in tandem with the other. It was important that I had two cat flaps that were operated by one key. This led to further letters and calls to the manufacturers as their flaps come supplied with the possibility of three different colour-coded collar keys. A supervisor at the local DIY store kindly opened up several boxes before finding one with the same coloured collar key as the one originally purchased. The manufacturers were helpful and supportive throughout.

J.S., Purley-on-Thames, Berkshire

Sibling Incest?

I have two cats, Tim and Suki, brother and sister, both neutered. Recently Tim has started mounting Suki as if to mate with her. After he realizes it's a futile pursuit, he stops and licks himself. Is this usual and should I try to stop him? Suki doesn't seem to mind. She just looks bored.

J.M., Bristol

Mounting is part of cat body language, and, like human kissing, can be social not sexual. "Cats don't have many ways of expressing their emotions, so they may mount each other when they feel excitement, stress or anger," says Peter Neville, cat behaviour expert. "Some spayed female cats seem to have a phantom season, and this could be setting Tim off." Thus Tim's behaviour could be either emotional or pseudo-sexual. Since Suki doesn't mind, there's no need to try to stop him.

Highly Sexed Cat

My three-year-old female cat was spayed at the age of six months. Since then every three months she has various callers and she completely changes from a home-loving cat to rather a wild one rolling around at the toms as if she were in heat. The toms try to mount her but without success. This lasts about three days, when the toms vanish and she reverts to her lovely loving self. Can you explain what is causing this?

L.B., Oulton Broad, Suffolk

Sometimes a spaying operation leaves a microscopic piece of ovarian tissue behind. "In this case, a cat will still come into season. A simple urine test will reveal if this has happened," explains Peter Neville, a cat behaviour counsellor. If a bit of ovary is left in the body, it could be taken out with a further operation. Sometimes, however, even properly spayed cats have a shadow cycle. "It is the hormones in the pituitary gland which trigger ovarian activity and these hormones are still produced even though they don't find their target. Nevertheless, the scent in the urine changes and the cats start calling and rolling."

Introducing a New Kitten

With the best intentions, my relations bought a tom tabby kitten, Buffy, now four months old, as company for their eighteen-month-old black-and-white spayed female, Tootsie. The mischievous young tom wants to play but she will not accept him on any terms. She behaves like an insulted dowager and hides from him. He hunts her down but faces unsheathed claws and spitting. What can be done?

W.P., Chester

It is early days in their relationship and I assume Tootsie is not causing Buffy any real harm. Once he is neutered he will start to calm down and they may end up as reasonable companions, if not friends.

"Give her lots of attention," suggests Claire Bessant of the Feline Advisory Bureau. "Don't shut them away from each other, but feed them nearby so that they have to share space. In cold weather they will want to be in the warmest place, so encourage them to sit in the same room."

If Tootsie's attacks are drawing blood, then perhaps she is one of those cats who is naturally solitary. In this case,

57

you may have to think again about re-homing one or other. "Dogs are pack animals and learn to get on with each other," says Claire Bessant. "Unfortunately cats aren't, and you can't force them to be sociable."

Sibling Rivalry

Bendigo, our Havana brown Siamese, lives with his sister, Baci, and they are both kept in at night with a litter tray. During the day the tray is taken away and they both seem happy to go outside. But Bendigo likes to pee on the duvet in each of the bedrooms. We have to keep the door of every upstairs room shut but at least once a week he manages to get in. What can we do?

F.F., Bradfield, Berkshire

Female cats, even spayed ones, are sometimes territorially possessive about areas where they might have kittens. Bendigo and Baci are not fighting but Bendigo is feeling the pressure from his sister and is trying anxiously to hang on to his territory, says Peter Neville, cat behaviour counsellor. "Therefore he is scentmarking in places where he feels he has greater security. This makes him feel more comfortable." Don't punish him because that will make him even more anxious. He needs his own space where Baci cannot follow him.

"Keep each cat in a separate room at night, or perhaps give Bendigo the airing cupboard," says Peter Neville. "You could put in an electronic cat flap, so that only he can get in and out during the day."

Worried Brothers

Ambrose and Harvey, our two neutered brother cats, have been messing in the house. The problem started after we had been away on holiday and left my parents to house-sit. The cats also come home with scratches and bits missing after fights with other cats in the neighbourhood. We successfully weaned them off the litter tray at three months.

M.R., Hurstpierpoint, Sussex

Your cats are marking their territory because they are stressed. Perhaps they were upset by your parents being in the house or by changes in their daily routine. They may also be anxious about a neighbouring cat who is beating them up. Leaving urine or faeces scentmarks reassures them. Clean the marked areas with biological washing liquid.

"Never punish them. This will just make them feel more stressed," warns Claire Bessant of the Feline Advisory Bureau. "Start by denying them access to rooms they have marked by shutting the doors, because they will have a natural urge to top up marked areas when the scent is fading. The doors must be shut for weeks, perhaps months. What starts as a reaction to stress can become a habit and then the feel of a sofa or bed can prompt them to do it again."

Do what you can to make the cats feel secure by keeping to a set routine and behaving calmly. If necessary, just keep them in the kitchen. If you think neighbouring feline bullies are worrying them, then you could restore the litter tray in the house. But if you do so, you will have to keep it available. Next time you go away, put them in a good cattery."

Litter Training, Litter Troubles and Cats and the Human Lavatory

How would you like it if you had about four square yards to use as a lavatory which was only flushed once a day or sometimes only every other day? You would pick your way through the area trying to find a square foot where you could go without fear of getting your shoes wet. It would be very off-putting. You might even decide to find somewhere else to go. Well, that's how your cat feels if you don't clean the litter tray out frequently enough.

A cat may stop using a litter tray simply because it is dirty. Like us, cats are clean animals, who like to attend to a call of nature in dry secure areas. They need somewhere to dig where they can be confident that their paws will stay clean. So a litter tray should be cleaned daily, or better still twice a day. Frequent cleaning is also the best way to reduce the smell of a tray. Besides, if there is more than one cat, and you are going to clean only once daily, then you need one tray per animal. Even with frequent cleaning, some cats won't go in the same litter tray as another animal, so you may have to have two trays just to cater to a cat's fastidious nature.

Some cats like to urinate in one place and defecate in another. Sure, they will use the litter tray for number one, but not number two (or vice versa). If this ties in with what is happening, try two litter trays, one for each purpose.

Finally, when a cat needs to go, it needs to feel safe. If one of your cats is being ambushed by its fellow pet when it enters or leaves the box, it will stop using it. A decent privacy is required too, so a tray in full view of everybody else, human or animal, in the house may not suit a shy feline.

Cats will stop using the litter tray if it has been

moved to a place which they consider unsuitable, unsafe or just plain wrong. In that case they may persist in using the old area, even though it no longer has a tray. Put it back! Then start slowly moving the tray inch by inch over several weeks to where you wish it to be.

Cats are fussy about the kind of litter they use. If a kitten has grown up using fuller's earth, for instance, it may flatly refuse to go on sawdust. Moreover, the larger the individual pieces of litter, the less popular they are among felines. Going into a box and having to shift the equivalent of cobblestones is not a feline's idea of a de luxe loo. In practice this means cats often prefer the most expensive kind of litter!

Covered trays are best for owners – they keep the smell in and stop the litter being scattered all over the floor. But some cats don't like them. So if you are considering changing to a covered tray, experiment with a cardboard box (with an entrance cut in it) to check the kitty will use it before spending money on the real thing.

Then there is the vexed question of cats who leave their bottoms outside the litter tray. Somehow they have lost the point of the litter. They dig, sometimes almost to Australia. Then, instead of turning round to put their bottom over the hole they have just made, they leave it hanging out over the edge. Persians, in particular, seem to have difficulty learning proper toilet behaviour. Ideally a kitten is taught by its mother how to use a litter tray but some Persians never seem to catch on. To compound the problem, faeces will sometimes be caught on the furry bottom of a long-haired cat and deposited outside, rather than inside, the litter tray. Simply clipping short the hair round the bottom will make this less likely to occur.

Many of the anguished letters sent to me are from owners whose cats are going in the wrong place (from the human point of view). This is often because, from a cat's point of view, the place that humans consider suitable (whether a litter tray indoors or the shrubbery out of doors) isn't suitable at all. Something is just wrong – the earth, the litter, or the geographical location.

Occasionally the underlying cause is stress. Cats under stress will sometimes leave their faeces on their owner's duvet, or start spraying urine on a vertical surface from an upright position. They have emotional or social difficulties – examples of this are to be found in Chapter Four.

Finally, don't forget that painful condition, common to both humans and cats, cystitis. Cystitis is often caused by crystals in the bladder. It causes cats to be caught short, so that they fail to reach the litter tray in time. If your cat is urinating frequently, passing blood in its urine, straining to urinate and sometimes crying with pain as it does so, it needs veterinary attention immediately. Cats, like humans, often suffer from recurring cystitis. With good veterinary treatment each episode can be cleared up quite quickly, but the cat may take a dislike to the litter tray. After all, it is when it is squatting in its tray that the burning symptoms of cystitis occur so it associates the tray with the pain. In this case, the cat may need not just good veterinary treatment, but retraining to the litter tray.

Some cats teach themselves to use washbasins and bath plug holes. How they know that these areas can be washed away I do not know. It is also possible to teach a cat to use the human lavatory. In America it is possible to buy the Kitty Whiz transfer system, a special plastic device which you put between the loo and the seat. You sprinkle litter on it and the cat uses it like a litter tray. After three weeks you cut a hole about three inches square in the middle of the plastic, still putting litter on the remaining paper. Widen the hole and after two months use no paper at all. Hey presto!! Your cat is now using the human lavatory. Well, that's the theory anyway. Next you need to teach it to flush. As some cats have learned to open doors by hanging on the door handle, this probably could be done! So please let me know if your cat pulls the chain!

Won't Use the Litter Tray

Sam, our tortoiseshell tabby, was a badly neglected stray who had been left outside to fend for himself when we took him in. He has always had a tray of earth, as he would not go near cat litter, and we leave it every time we go out and at night. He has spent pennies in it but will not do anything more. We come home to find the carpet by the door torn up and him waiting to dash out. He uses a place under the rhododendrons at the top of the garden. He's taken to the vet regularly and is in good health. Can you suggest anything.

E.S., Sutton, Surrey

Sam's owners have already done one thing right – giving him soil instead of commercial litter. A cat which has been living rough sometimes just won't change from earth to litter. Installing a cat flap may solve the problem by allowing Sam free access outdoors. But his owners are reluctant to have one, because there are a lot of stray toms in the area who invade people's houses through the cat flap.

Sam has been checked with the vet so there is no medical reason for the problem. His early life as a stray has taught him to "go" outside. "He has such a strong association with using the outside that he just has to get out," says Sarah Heath, vet and pet behaviour counsellor. She points out that defecation takes longer than urination so cats feel particularly vulnerable at this time. She suggests covering the litter tray, to see if that gives Sam a greater feeling of security.

Sometimes cats want the tray completely covered and sometimes they just want three high sides and an open top. Experiment with a cardboard box. Placing some earth from under the rhododendrons in the tray may attract Sam with its familiar scent. Try adding a second tray full of earth, in case Sam is one of those cats who will not defecate in the same place as they urinate. Again, mix some earth from underneath the rhododendrons.

There can be very individual reasons why cats have difficulties with litter trays. If none of these suggestions works, ask your vet to refer you to a pet behaviour counsellor.

In the Gravel

Our three kittens, Lotte, Homes and Ben, have outgrown their litter tray but are now using our sitting-patio area in the garden. Its pea-grit gravel is ideal for their purposes but with hot summer days coming up, it's getting a bit smelly. Have you got some suggestions on how we get them to do it elsewhere?

S.D., Coulsdon, Surrey

When cats defecate or urinate outside, they need to feel secure. Your kittens have chosen a place near the house where they probably feel safe because it's close to you. To persuade them to go in a different area, you need to offer them an even nicer spot. Choose a place which will seem secure to them – not too near the neighbour's cats' territory, underneath shrubs or sheds – and put down some dry matter like peat, or sand. It needs to be a dryish area. Then scoop up some of their solid matter, as much as possible, from the gravel and install it there, so that your chosen spot smells like a latrine to them. Keep adding this until they are doing it there. This should work if you choose the right place and if they feel secure in it.

At the same time, make the gravel less hospitable by keeping it as damp as possible with a garden hose each evening and morning. You could try Scoot, etc. Or you could try feeding them in the gravel area. They don't like defecating where they dine.

Don't put them off indoor litter completely. You may need them to use a tray if they are ill or on bonfire night. If all else fails, change the pea-grit to a larger gravel. Cats don't like having to dig in what is, to them, the equivalent of cobblestones.

Won't Use the Cat Flap

We have just had a cat flap fitted through our kitchen wall for our two cats Bailey and Smudge. It's about a foot deep and they have taken to going through the tunnel, but we have to prop open the flap on the outer wall. How can we make them come through it closed?

S.D., West Wickham, Kent

Some cats are better at learning to open a cat flap than others. "Prop the flap open fully, then less and less, so that they get used to increasing the pressure to open it," says cat behaviour counsellor Peter Neville. "Take this slowly over a period of time. What you mustn't ever do is just shove the cat through." Usually cats open the cat flap by pressing with a front paw and the side of the cheek. It's just possible that your tunnel is too narrow for them to do this. "Check how easy the outside flap is," Peter Neville advises. "See if you can get something very light like a thin sheet of plastic."

Bottom over the Edge

Geraldine, our Persian cat, does not know how to use a litter tray. She goes to the litter tray, digs a hole in the centre with her paws, then does it over the side. She attempts to cover up the mess by scratching the lino. How do we train her?

B.C., Manchester

Try a covered litter tray. To make sure she will use one, before buying, experiment with a cardboard box over the old tray. Most cats will accept a covered tray. When you take it home, fill the new tray with litter from the old, making sure some soiled litter is among it. This makes it more likely that Geraldine will accept the new arrangement. When she is digging in a covered tray, she cannot leave her bottom over the edge. For some reason Persians are notoriously bad at using litter trays.

Our fourteen-year-old cat, Polly, presented us with the same problem as that posed by Geraldine, leaving her bottom outside the litter tray. Providing a larger covered tray did not help, unfortunately. She just left her bottom out of the entrance. Our eventual solution, which works well, was to place a smaller tray inside the larger one, producing a gap of two-and-a-half inches or so at the entrance. This ensures that Polly has to step across the gap to enter and use the inner tray. Any overspill is absorbed by a small amount of litter placed in the gap area. This method has worked well for the last two years, since Polly decided she preferred indoors to the great outdoors!

D.G., Penn, Buckinghamshire

I had the same problem with my cat Mitzi, who left her bottom outside the tray. I bought a deep, round washing-up bowl to replace the low-sided litter tray. The cat was unable to get her tail and rear end over the side. The arrangement had other advantages in that the bowl was easier to lift with its rounded rim and was also easier to keep clean. Mitzi took to it like a cat to litter!

J.W., Kettering, Northamptonshire

War against Smelly Litter

I really hate the smell of a cat litter box, yet I have to have one. My cats live indoors in a flat without a garden. Any suggestions?

M.L., South-east London

Clean the cat litter twice a day or more. Frequent cleaning keeps the smell to a minimum. Theoretically (I have never tried this) you can teach your cats to use the human loo. You place the litter tray in the lavatory with an old loo seat round it. Over several weeks, you put first one, then two, then more telephone directories under the tray, making sure the cats are used to the height before raising the tray higher. When the tray is at the right level – at the same height as the real loo seat – put the litter tray (still with its spare seat) on top of the lavatory. Let the cats use the tray on top of the lavatory till they are used to it. Finally, take away the tray.

To reduce smell from the litter tray I place a number of sheets of newspaper flat on the bottom of the tray and litter on top of them. If the cat does a tinkle, I wait awhile then ease the clean part of the litter on to another newspaper, fold the paper in the litter tray with the urine inside and place this in a plastic carrier bag. Then I place the fresh paper back into the tray with some extra litter. There is never any smell because the urine soaks into the paper which absorbs the smell. If the cat does a dirty I just fold the entire amount up into all the newspaper and put *all* in a plastic bag then start afresh.

B.J., West London

We have found the answer to the problem of concealing a cat litter tray. When we had our kitchen redesigned, we posed the problem to our architect and builder, both fortunately ailurophiles. They came up with the perfect solution – use a standard base cupboard unit, at the end of a run, to house the litter tray and cut a cat-size opening in the blank end. The cats have privacy, one can open the cupboard door to remove the tray for cleaning, and no one is aware that there is a cat loo in the kitchen (as long as one cleans it frequently)!

S.G., Gravesend, Kent

This is an ingenious solution to a common problem. All too often cat-hating guests in the kitchen are put off their meal by the sight of the litter tray in use.

Cats and the Human Lavatory

I enclose a photo of my cat Tensingh using the loo. She was never taught to use it, but whilst we prepared for bed, so did she. Her twin, Henry, never used the loo. She is nineteen-and-a-half years old now and no longer feels safe on the lavatory rim, so we provide her with a litter tray.

R.M., Evesham, Worcestershire

Cats can indeed be trained to use the human loo. My two Burmese cats are now nine years old and live with free access to the outdoors. For the first four years of their life, however, they lived indoors in an airy first floor flat with access to the open air via a screened balcony. After the training with telephone directories, they used the loo all the time from the age of seven months. The decision to look after cats indoors was taken after a chance meeting in Regent's Park with an American animal psychologist at Harvard. She provided comprehensive evidence, scientific and anecdotal, that with careful planning and consideration cats can be looked after indoors without detriment to their well-being and development – and without recourse to smelly litter boxes. Some cats in New York have apparently even been trained to flush the loo after use. Interestingly, having used the great outdoors exclusively for several years, when the weather became exceptionally wet and cold this winter both cats reverted to using our loo for the odd occasion.

E.B., North London

My Siamese, Sirikiat, who died three years ago aged nearly twenty, used our loo on two occasions. Although she had the complete freedom of our garden, there was snow on the ground which she didn't like very much when this occurred. I would not have believed this if I hadn't seen her myself. Needless to say she did not flush on either occasion.

D.T., Barry, Vale of Glamorgan

Our cat Mungo, though not at all confined to the house, frequently chooses to use the plug hole in the bath or hand basin rather than going outside. He squats very neatly right over the hole, making it easy to flush away. In fact, he has been known to come in from the garden especially to use the bath and frequently accompanies me when I go to the loo. I must add he is completely self-taught. I am not sure how you would set about training a cat to do this. He is a great character – one of his tricks is jumping up to pull down a door handle, thus opening the door in one easy movement. He hasn't yet figured out how to turn knob-type handles but I am sure he is working on it.

S.D., Sherborne, Dorset

Yes it is possible and relatively easy to train your cat to use a lavatory. In the States one can buy a special paper for it. What you do is put the paper between the loo and the seat and sprinkle litter on it. After three weeks, cut a hole about three inches square in the middle of the paper, still putting cat litter on the remaining paper. Continue to widen the hole periodically and eventually, after about two months, use no paper at all. The cat will have become so used to using the toilet that it will continue to do so. One has to see it to believe it but the end result is well worth the time invested. Cleaning up while training is also simple – just lift the toilet seat and the cat waste just falls in.

P.H., West London

Litter Allergy
My white cat, Sophie, has a recurring problem where dust from her litter tray irritates one or other of her eyes, which she then rubs with a paw until the eye almost closes up. My vet confirms there is no infection and has suggested I try different types of litter but I cannot find any product which does not trouble her. Can you suggest one?

M.W-O., Aberdeen

White cats (and dogs for that matter) seem particularly prone to allergies. Try a cat litter made entirely of straw (see Appendix Three). Incidentally, this is also a good litter for house rabbits. If this doesn't work, try washed builders' sand.

For many years I have used Irish moss peat in my cats' litter trays. It is clean and dust free and, when soiled matter is removed, can be put straight on to the garden. There is also a litter made from waste paper which is dust free. I have found it good.

M.B., Hereford

For some time I had either a cat with pink paws or clouds of dust flying everywhere. My cats refused to use paper or wood products, preferring the carpet. I solved the problem by buying a large cheap bag of potting compost. The cats were keen to use it and disposal was easy for me as I emptied it on to the garden. The solids are not so easily removed and it has to be changed more frequently but the compost is recycling on the garden.

P.D., Worthing, West Sussex

Computerized Litter Tray

I have heard of a special cat litter box, almost self-cleaning and electrically operated. My daughter was injured in an accident two years ago and is in almost constant pain so that all daily tasks are very difficult. Sometimes her help doesn't turn up and one of her problems is her beloved cat's litter tray. I have tried to track this new box down as I think it could be a great help to her. Can you give me any information about it?

J.S., South-west London

There is a self-cleaning litter box sold in America which claims it is for people who "Never Want To Touch, Toss,

Turn Or Scoop Your Cat's Litter Again". *With the help of readers I have tracked this down. It is quite expensive and as I have not tried it myself I cannot vouch for its efficiency.*

Readers have suggested three other possibilities – disposable litter trays which are just thrown away when used; a cardboard cat litter house which is thrown away after twelve days; or using any cat litter which clumps so well that the waste can be picked out while leaving the rest of the litter.

Regarding the computerized kitty litter box . . . An old friend in Los Angeles bought one for her many Californian cats. Although initially she thought her cats would be frightened by the automatic working, she subsequently wrote to me that the cats were so fascinated by the mechanical combing action that they appeared to be eating more than usual, in order to load the kitty litter tray up so they could sit around the machine and watch it work.

R.F., Empuriabrava, Spain

I am disabled and find certain tasks difficult, sometimes impossible. My cat has a cat flap and prefers to go out whenever possible but for emergencies I have devised the following: a thick wad of newspaper overlapping both ends in the litter tray, and screwed-up newspaper in the litter tray above it. I pick up both ends of newspaper together, hence no spillage etc., and have a bin liner alongside. I have done this for a number of years very satisfactorily.

K.L., Cullompton, Devon

Breaking and Entering, Cat Burglars and the Raffles of Cat Crime

Duncan Doughnuts, a handsome tabby-and-white moggy in Bath, started the *Telegraph*'s competition for Cat Burglar of the Year, probably the first ever competition of this kind. Duncan, luckily for the birds and beasts of Bath, hadn't really got the hang of proper hunting. After bringing home one or two worms and frogs, he decided to concentrate on the socially responsible work of picking up litter.

"He brings in rubbish such as old bus passes and cigarette packets," explained his owner. "He forages in the compost heap and last month dragged in (through the cat flap) a four-foot long rose branch, covered in thorns. At Christmas he brought in a strange (to us) catnip mouse, which he probably stole from a neighbouring cat!"

Except for the fact that it was a *catnip* mouse, Duncan was behaving as lots of cats do – bringing home his prey. But why do cats insist on showing us what they have caught? One theory, probably not true, is that they are bringing the prey home in order to teach us to hunt. In their eyes we are huge and inadequate kittens who have never learned what to do with a mouse. Again and again, they bring home a tasty meal, and again and again, we disappoint them by refusing to eat it!

A more likely, though less funny, explanation is that cats bring their prey into the house because it is a safe place for them to eat. This, of course, makes sense when the prey is edible. But cats like Duncan are bringing back inedible prey.

Duncan was not the only *Telegraph* cat with a bizarre idea of how to hunt. His confession of theft brought in a flood of letters about thieving cats. Many modern cats, it seems, have become soft in their outlook. Instead of slaughtering mice and birds, they sneak out at night to track down fluffy toys, raid golf courses for balls, swipe sausages still hot from the neighbour's barbecue, steal gold pencils, take men's underpants from strange bedrooms, and even occasionally bring home a mink stole.

Interestingly, the cats who have taken up this cuddly version of hunting, are often oriental breeds or long-haired cats. They also have owners who perhaps unwittingly encourage this behaviour by praising them for it and showing evident amusement. Ordinary non-pedigree moggies are more likely to bring home living prey.

What amuses me most is that the *Daily Telegraph* is a conservative newspaper, on the side of law and order, tough on crime and less interested in the causes of crime. Its letter writers often favour capital punishment for murderers and prison sentences for thieves. But somehow these feelings never apply to the owners of stealing cats. The letters showed that perfectly respectable law-abiding people were proud of their cats' appalling behaviour. They wrote shamelessly boasting about the swag their cats brought in, vying with each other over the size and value of stolen goods. Admittedly most of the owners tried to return valuable items, when they could find the owner. Open days, when neighbours can come and view the loot and claim their belongings, might be the answer when the victims of crime cannot be tracked down. Luckily, most neighbours seemed to see the funny side of being a victim of feline crime.

The proud winner of the title *Daily Telegraph* Cat Burglar of 1996 was an eight-year-old lilac Burmese cat, Minnimore, the Raffles of cat crime. From the age of two Minnimore had specialized in breaking and entering into other people's houses. Mainly he stole cuddly toys, but occasionally he would be tempted by clothes or kitchen items.

"The whole thing is extremely embarrassing, as you can imagine. We go round the neighbourhood knocking on doors to see if we can find the owners of the stolen goods," admitted his owners. "But for the vast majority we have been unable to find where they come from, which suggests that Minnimore ranges over a far wider area than we had always assumed would be the case."

Articles brought home by Minnimore included a pincushion, three feather dusters all with two-foot long handles, two separate bedroom slippers, a polo-neck jersey, a long black evening glove, a fur tippet, a fur hat, numerous socks and a kitchen cushion. His cuddly toy collection included Cuthbert the Camel, a kookaburra, a dinosaur, six teddy bears, three bunny rabbits, a Mickey Mouse, a koala, a gorilla, a skunk, a whale, a panda, a musical tortoise and a glove puppet in the shape of a bear.

After he appeared in my column, Minnimore became famous. He appeared on a television programme and was psychoanalyzed by a cat behaviour expert who (just like a social worker) blamed his upbringing for his antisocial behaviour. Unlike ordinary cats, Minnimore revelled in the attention. "He acted like a real trouper and enjoyed the whole day's filming enormously," reported his owner at the time.

As an aid to moral reformation, Minnimore was given a large cat aerobic centre. The idea was that he would rush up and down this, using up his energy on healthy exercise rather than thieving. To fulfil his hunting instincts, his food was hidden in the house rather than just given to him openly. The hope was that he would hunt for it, rather than cuddly toys.

Further publicity followed. Minnimore appeared, surrounded by his cuddly toy trophies, in another national newspaper and even as far away as a magazine in South Africa. But the publicity and the strenuous efforts at reforming him, did no good at all. Perhaps he just enjoyed it all too much.

"After a year's good conduct Minnimore has been displaying severe recidivist tendencies," reported his owner in 1998. "We have now acquired two teddies, two stuffed Dalmatians, one elephant, one water buffalo, and one chameleon. During one evening he brought in six items of booty, one straight after the other, including a bedroom slipper. We feel particularly badly about the chameleon because it has a lover's message on its shop tag – 'This is for a gorgeous darling who I love more than anything.' "

Marmite and Earwig

I came home from work one day to find, inexplicably, an extremely dirty sponge on the hall floor. The next day I found another even dirtier sponge torn to shreds on my bed. Later the explanation came from an annoyed neighbour. He had been painting the outside of his house and twice when he had put down the sponge he used for mopping up drips our cat Marmite had nipped into his garden and stolen it. There was much joking about Marmite being a sponger and that, we thought, was that.

My flatmate and I witnessed a remarkable sight. Coming along the garden wall was my cat Marmite, with her boyfriend, Earwig, carrying between them a piece of polystyrene packaging about two feet long! This they proudly deposited at our feet – the ultimate sponge. I have never before or since seen cats working together in this way. Where they had got it from and how far they had carried it together I have no idea, but it must have taken a fair degree of co-operation and determination on their part.

H.C., Ruthin, Denbighshire

Ranji and Mrs Guthrie

Ranji, the Siamese I had the pleasure of belonging to many moons ago, on one occasion pinched the kipper off the plate of the good lady next door, Mrs Guthrie. She had gone to open her front door. He brought it in and placed it on my lap. My poor mother had to deal with a hysterical woman who had just seen Ranji disappearing over the garden fence complete with kipper when she returned to the kitchen for her Sunday morning breakfast.

J.L., Thames Ditton, Surrey

Underpants

My neighbour stopped me as I got home and said she had seen Timmy come from a house at the bottom of the road carrying what looked like a piece of cloth. When I went in, I found a pair of underpants in the hall . . . Our friends opposite had a cat-chasing dog and Timmy saw this as a challenge. He would dash into the house, pinch a dog biscuit, and run home with it, leaving a barking collie at the closed gate. Then we moved and for a time Timmy was too busy establishing his territory to go thieving.

His first offering was a small Yorkshire pudding, and this gift was repeated each Sunday. His last effort came when he was only a week or so from dying. He brought me a warm, freshly baked fairy cake and crumbled it on the kitchen floor. I told him off for stealing, and for making a mess. He shot me one of his looks, went out and brought me another.

B.W., Southwold, Suffolk

Autumn Leaves

Since he was a kitten, Casey has always been a cat who collects and brings in through the cat flap a wide assortment of objects. Autumn is greeted with a wild determination to ensure that all the fallen leaves are rounded up and stored in the kitchen instead of blowing skittishly in the garden. His look of sheer exhaustion pleads, "Well, you could help me, you know – there are plenty more to be collected!" Without question, though, Casey's forte is plastic bags of every shape, colour and size, some with very questionable contents.

Casey was particularly friendly with old George next door and the pair would spend many a happy hour together in George's shed. One day George watched Casey stroll casually into the shed, jump up on to the work top, have a good rummage around, select a large plastic bag containing assorted screws, secure it firmly in his mouth and promptly leave the shed. With determination and the customary howling to announce his latest catch, he managed to drag his prize out of the garden, along the road, down our drive and into the kitchen. Needless to say Casey got a cuddle to show appreciation for his efforts and George did get his screws back.

L.B., Whitstable, Kent

Stocking the Pond

We built a pond and our cat, Claude, stocked it for us. Every night for several nights he tootled in through the cat flap with fish from some neighbour's pond, we know not whose. They ranged in size from tiddler goldfish to large koi carp. All were unharmed and are doing well.

L.M., Aldershot, Surrey

Grass Balls

I used to go across to feed my neighbour's cat, Thomasina, when they were on holiday. Though my neighbour told me beforehand that Thomasina brought in lumps of grass, it in no way prepared me for what I was going to see – to wit: perfectly round balls of tiny grass cuttings, the size of tennis balls!

The moment you tried to pick them up, they crumbled into thousands of tiny bits of grass. I still can't think how she got them into a round ball shape in the first place, how she got her mouth round them, and how she got them back through the cat door. Finally, how did she put them down on the floor without them disintegrating?

G.D., Leafield, Oxfordshire

Baby's Gloves

I have a Birman, Crackers, who has stopped bringing me things, but I used to have a cupboard devoted to all the items he brought me – white furry earmuffs, a white-and-blue jumper, two unrelated gloves, a teddy bear, various sports socks, a football scarf, a half-finished knitted sleeve, another half-finished front or back in the same colour wool, and two baby's gloves knotted together.

P.C., Rugby, Warwickshire

Balls of Wool

Our Birman cat, Blue, is addicted to mohair wool and has frequently brought balls of it in. He once stole one from our next-door neighbour and as he returned home the ball was unwinding behind him, leaving a twisting and turning trail for some thirty yards in the bushes between our gardens, with our friendly neighbour hanging on to the other end, laughing and saying, "Now will you believe me?" Blue at one time came in with the knitted-up back of somebody's mohair jumper. Another time, somebody's mohair knitting lay across a dividing back garden wall for weeks without being claimed. Only we knew how it got there. Thank goodness mohair is out of fashion now.

B.D., Bolton le Sands, Lancashire

Laying in Kindling

One of my cats, Floppsy alias Pearl, always without fail for the past four years brings in wood and sticks when the weather starts getting colder. She started doing this, as if to gain favour and praise, when she saw me bringing wood and sticks for the wood-burning stove four years ago. When we see the pile of sticks on the doorstep or on the floor in the kitchen just inside the cat flap, we know that it is getting colder and that we need to light the stove. She does this on a nightly basis, never missing a night of labour when autumn arrives. At the crack of dawn she can be seen with quite large pieces of bark or stick in her mouth. She carries them from the wooded area of our two-acre garden. Her nightly endeavours keep me in kindling. I believe she does it as an act of love to help me. She meows at me every morning and beckons me to her offering, to which I respond with praise and affection. I believe this reinforces her behaviour.

A.A., Westbury-sub-Mendip, Somerset

Toy Mice

My name is Daniel. I am ten years old and I have two cats called Rocky and Rambo. They are black and white and brothers. Rambo has brought in a variety of things including two toy mice, one wooden and one soft, an immense amount of pond weed, corned beef sandwiches, a pirate hat, and plastic sheeting. Rocky specializes in live prey. His best catch ever was a foot-long koi carp.

D.A., Nottingham

Frogspawn

My favourite pussy present to date was a large helping (about a mugful) of frogspawn from the next-door pond. It was too much to carry in his mouth so Domino must have dragged it along the ground then through the cat flap.

M.B., Harpenden, Hertfordshire

Racing Pigeons

Our three-year-old tabby, Tabitha, has brought us numerous tennis balls from the ten-year-old boy who lives next door but one. Tabitha has to come over two walls which are about five feet high. Shuttlecocks and cleaning rags have been presented through the cat flap. A koi carp at least nine inches long and very chunky came from a pond three walls away. A racing pigeon, a man's thermal short-sleeved vest, and twice she brought us a slipper.

K.S., Taunton, Somerset

Fresh Cream Cake

We don't think Duncan Doughnut's efforts are up to the standards achieved by Tipsy, the beloved Siamese we owned when we first married. One Saturday she returned bringing with her an individual fresh cream cake (a sponge drop) still in its blue-and-white paper case.

S.A., Market Rasen, Lincolnshire

81

Frozen Chicken

Blot, a long-haired black cat, once appeared at the top of the garden dragging something behind him, sometimes straddling it like a leopard taking an impala up a tree. With much effort he reached our back door. His prey was a three-and-a-half pound supermarket frozen chicken, in its plastic wrapper.

D.C., Rhiw, Gwynedd

Looking after Baby

TuTu, our long-departed but still lovingly remembered Siamese, was fascinated by our baby. The cat was intrigued by the feeding process for Stephen, who was bottle fed, and loved to sit and watch. One day, TuTu came through the cat door carrying a baby's teat in his mouth, which he laid on the floor for us. At first we thought it was one of the teats from Stephen's bottle, but then we realized it was a slightly different style, and must have come from somewhere else. While our son was being bottle fed, TuTu regularly contrived to locate and retrieve teats. We can only guess that he was able to get into another house nearby where there was also a baby. We had visions of some other mother being driven frantic by the disappearance of her supply of bottle teats!

J. and M.S., Exeter, Devon

Stuffed Owl

Charlie, a large ginger tom owned by my late aunt, brought home – among other things – a small jewellery drawer from an Edwardian dressing table (empty); a jumper on knitting needles plus the ball of wool; a live goldfish and a stuffed owl.

A.F., Weymouth, Dorset

Plastic Gorilla

Measle dragged, through the hedge and along our two hundred foot garden, a young girl's swimsuit. A spin in the washer proved it to be yellow and to have a complete motif of Disney's Cinderella. A few days later came a man's pair of striped pants. Next day a man's sock. Its pairing came the next day. It's autumn. The latest arrival is a plastic gorilla. Who knows what winter will bring forth?

J.S., Shoreham-by-Sea, Sussex

Cat Collar Magnets
A friend's cat brought in four cat collars that had the magnets on them for opening cat doors. We still wonder how she got them off the cats' necks!

A.B., North London

Fried Fish
Our Siamese cat, Thai-moon, had a penchant for bringing us wrapped sweets, held by the end of the paper twist. He also brought a rather dilapidated teddy bear (probably discarded), chop bones, and a lovely piece of fried fish, still warm – he ate and enjoyed that himself. One day not long before Christmas he brought us a large, very pregnant white mouse – the next day he brought four more. We had to buy a mouse cage for them as we didn't know where they came from. Eventually as he was off to get another one, my husband spotted him entering a shed some distance away. It transpired he had discovered them in an aquarium with box lid on top, which he removed.

C.M., Exeter, Devon

Mink Stole

My Siamese cat dragged a mink stole through the cat flap. He had pulled it all over the muddy garden and we had to apologize to our neighbour for the mess it was in. He at least knew a good thing when he saw one.

M.P., Pulborough, Sussex

Fresh Steak

I am mightily relieved to hear of other thieving cats. Furball of Bath, a long-furred black cat (perfect for passing undetected at night) has picked on one house in particular (two iron gates, two walls, a road and a fence away), diligently bringing home all the furry toys he can find – sometimes two or more journeys in one night. Our neighbour has grown quite used to the sound of Furball rootling around her ground floor until he has found a trophy worth filching. All stolen property is returned through her letter box the next morning.

His companion, Cinders, now too old to jump walls, in her youth broke the top six inches of a wooden fence at the bottom of my garden when returning hastily from our neighbour's kitchen. Though always a heavy cat, I suspect that the fence snapped due to the additional weight of a steak in her mouth, garnished but as yet un-cooked.

J.G., Bath

Flowers

My cat Zara is a tabby Siamese seal point. Right from kitten age, she has brought me lamb chops, a joint of cooked meat, seagull's feathers, sponges, a ball of string, and flowers from my neighbours' gardens. "You don't bring me flowers," as the song goes, but Zara does.

L.H., Torquay, Devon

Mouse in Trap

Re cats' offerings! One of mine once brought home a mouse – in the trap. I wondered who had spent ages seeking the trap.

J.T., Enfield, Middlesex

Fridge Burglar

Siamese are very ingenious and our cat Henry was so good at opening cupboards that not only did we have to have a child lock on the fridge to prevent him raiding the bacon, but we also had to fix one on the neighbour's fridge for the same reason.

R.M., Evesham, Worcestershire

Disgusted of Nuneaton

You reported on cats' retrieval of valuable items. I wonder if your sense of humour is shared with the original owners of these items, particularly the owners of the stolen koi carp, which could well have cost several hundred pounds. It appears from several small studies that domestic cats retrieve on average one small mammal or songbirds per month. If this is so, Britain's cats account for between 80,000,000 to 100,000,000 such animals a year. Perhaps you find these antics equally irresistible and worth of honourable mention. I, on the other hand, am surprised and not a little angered by your casually flippant attitude to feline behaviour.

P.P. Nuneaton, Warwickshire.

Wandering Cats, Indoor Cats, Foxy Encounters and Cats who Leave Home

The purring pussy cat who sleeps so calmly on the hearth rug is a wild lone hunter when he leaves the house. An energetic pet cat may spend many hours pursuing his own business in the next-door gardens, the field across the street, the roof tops of the local factory and the messy back yard of the neighbourhood garage. Some country cats go on long safaris through the fields, away for hours at a time.

Urban cats often two-time their owners. With a cat flap which allows them to come and go as they please, they may breakfast with their official owners, mooch down the street for elevenses four doors away, pop in for lunch with the housewife four streets away and finish up having tea with the old gentleman opposite. Then they come home for their supper looking as if they haven't had a bite all day. Cats are territorial animals but are flexible about territory size. If food is short, a single cat may have a territory as large as a hundred hectares, and like Rudyard Kipling's character will be a cat who walks by himself. But when there is plenty to eat, the same-sized territory may contain up to two thousand cats, forming quite close-knit colonies.

In the wild, males and females share their territory, though the dominant males will often harass young or less successful males. In his attempts to keep off competitors, an un-neutered tomcat may roam over a territory ten times greater than that of a female cat. So, if you want your cat to be a homebody, make sure you neuter him. Even so, a neutered or spayed pet can still have a territory of a square mile according to its temperament and the number of interlocking cat territories nearby.

Both the long-range hunters patrolling for up to a mile and the social butterflies popping in and out of other people's homes are equally worrying for their owners. Devoted cat lovers may find themselves virtually ignored most of the day and (if the cat flap isn't closed in the evening) deserted during the night as well. Puss pops in for his meals with the air of a man who is far too busy to spend much time with his family. Some of the dangers of this free come-and-go lifestyle are obvious. Traffic is the single most likely reason why cats fail to return home. An enormous number of cats are killed outright on the roads which is why, alas, it makes sense to talk to road sweepers if you have lost a cat. They may have seen a corpse. Other cats are merely wounded. Sometimes they drag themselves into a hedge and die. Others survive for longer and may be picked up and taken to a vet by kindly passers-by who then adopt them. Most vets' surgeries will give emergency aid to unidentified cat casualties and from the surgery, if nobody claims them, the survivors are usually rehomed by one of the animal charities.

Night time is danger time for cats. They have better vision in the twilight or the light of distant street lamps than we do, even if they can't see in pitch black. However, it takes cats up to an hour to adapt their sight from dim to bright, or bright to dim. Car lights, therefore, utterly blind them, which is one reason for the high number of feline road casualties. So the single most important way to keep your cat safe is to shut the cat flap during the night. This will also save the lives of the birds who feed on the ground mainly at dawn and dusk.

In some countries, cats face the risk of attack by larger predators. Luckily in Britain the only risk comes from foxes, who will only attack vulnerable cats – the young, the very old or the sick. Even so, a study in the Bristol area showed that less than one per cent of cats are killed by foxes, far fewer than those killed by traffic. Most of the victims are under the age of six months and when foxes do eat adult cats, it is probably only those already dead or seriously wounded by traffic.

The other danger that faces urban or suburban cats comes from human neighbours. It is just as disgusting for keen gardeners to find their flower beds full of cat faeces as it is for passers-by to find the pavement littered with dog poo. Yet the British habit of withdrawing the litter tray and expecting the cat to use the great outdoors positively encourages justified cat rage. The result is that angry people deliberately harm cats with poison, air guns or even traps.

The only way to keep your cat utterly safe is to put high fences round your garden and build a huge cat cage in it, or turn him into a totally indoor cat. My opinion, not shared by everybody, is that a cat's extra happiness in freedom is worth some risk, and that a cat should only be kept indoors if a human is there most of the day, if there is a companion cat, if the cat is elderly or infirm, or if some other exceptional circumstances make indoor life compulsory.

The final risk of freedom, not so much to your cat as to your own happiness, is that your cat will pack up and leave home if he feels he is happier elsewhere. Some cats merely arrange their lives so that they have a daytime home (when their true owners are out at work) and a night-time one. Others leave home for good, if there is stress at home from other cats or dogs.

There is a particular danger of losing your cat if you move to a house only a small distance away. For cats, though happy to live as part of the family, are usually attached primarily to territory, and only secondarily, unlike dogs, to individuals. Sometimes, when a house is sold, the cat is sold with it – an arrangement which suits the cat perfectly well if the incoming family is loving and caring. Long moves are usually successful if you keep your cat indoors for at least three or more weeks, making sure he is thoroughly at home in the new house as his core territory. But with small moves of only a mile or two, the cat may find his way back to his old territory, perhaps by smell, perhaps by some sixth homing sense which we, as humans, do not properly understand.

Two-timing Oliver

Two years ago we bought a four-month-old black-tipped shorthair cat, Oliver. He proved to be everything we could ask for in a cat. He is intelligent, affectionate, friendly to a fault and extremely handsome. He has company virtually all day, as my partner is at home most of the time and converses with him regularly. Ollie has a cat flap and can come and go as he pleases. To begin with we used to lock the cat flap at night to keep him in, but then he began to come home later and later, and this became impossible without staying up all night waiting for him – worse than a teenager.

The trouble is that we now rarely see Ollie. He comes home at meal times, demands to be fed heartily, and then disappears – sometimes for a few hours, sometimes for twelve hours, sometimes for eighteen hours or longer. This is both worrying and disappointing, as Ollie is extremely good company when he *is* around. We are fairly sure he has a second home – but it is impossible to track him, as the area is highly residential and full of hedges, walls and fences!

Do you have any idea at all what we can do to get him to live at home again? He is never ignored, he wants for nothing, and he seems blissfully happy. We do miss him such a lot but are terrified that if we attempt to lock him in, when he does go out he'll never return. Do we just have to accept the situation?

A.H., Poole, Dorset

If you think your Ollie is being fed elsewhere, put a note on his collar (if he has one) asking the people to ring you. When they do so, you can ask them not to welcome him in their home or at least not to feed him at all.

The best way to reduce wandering is by shutting the cat indoors at night. This is anyway what the Cats Protection League and the Feline Advisory Bureau recommend for all cats living near roads, since most accidents happen in the dark. Feed a main meal (reducing the amount at other times if necessary) just before you lock them in, otherwise they won't be there to lock in! Don't leave food down for them at any other time. If they want to eat, they have to turn up at this correct time. If the cat is not very interested in food, try giving a preliminary treat of prawns or a small piece of raw pig or ox heart, before the main meal. Only give this at the correct time – i.e. increase their incentive to come in. Cats get used to this quite quickly. "You could also feed the cats three or four times during the day at set regular times," suggests Claire Bessant of the FAB. They would then have to come in for each meal, making it less likely they will go on long-range patrol.

Curbing Wanderlust

Can you suggest how I can curb the wanderlust of my twenty-month-old spayed female Tonkinese cat, Cass? She is electronically tagged but of course this is no help unless she is taken as a lost pet to a vet or cat rescue. What might help is a radio transmitter so that I can track down where she actually goes to. Is such a thing possible or practicable for a period?

V.P., Thetford, Norfolk

You could buy a transmitter for your cat's collar, with a receiver and a directional antenna, but it will cost several hundred pounds for this and its batteries. But the device only works in open country or suburban areas. Large buildings block or reflect the signals. This equipment is mainly sold to wildlife researchers and falconers and you will have to practise to make proper use of it. The range is a few hundred yards. For one-off use it is probably too expensive and difficult to use, though it would be just what you need if you wanted to do a proper study of your cat's behaviour outside the home.

Collaring Eiger

My young cat, Eiger, is now eighteen months old. I would like to be a responsible owner and put a collar with a name tag on her. She, however, does not wish to be a responsible cat. Any suggestions?

A.R., Milford Haven, Pembrokeshire

I don't like collars for cats, even the kind with an elastic insert, because every year scores of unlucky cats catch their front paw in their collars and sometimes turn up at cat shelters with the collar cutting deeply into the flesh of the neck. There are special collars which are safer (see Appendix Three), but I favour microchipping cats at a vet's surgery at the time of neutering and spaying. This will mean your cat is identified if it ends up at an animal shelter, although it doesn't help ordinary people trace a stray cat who turns up at their home.

If Eiger has never worn a collar before, it may be difficult getting him used to it. "It's easiest to get a cat to wear a collar from an early age. Older cats sometimes go berserk in a collar for the first time," says Claire Bessant of the Feline Advisory Bureau. "To train them to wear one, you need to lay in a store of treats like prawns. Put on the collar for a minute or two and give a couple of

prawns, then take the collar off. Do this at a quiet moment in a room where the cat can't run off in panic. Keep doing this until the cat associates the collar with prawns!" Some cats will realize the collar isn't dangerous fairly soon; others may take weeks to get used to the idea. Don't hurry the process or the cat will get too stressed. You will have to be patient.

Lost, Stolen or Strayed

We went on holiday in July leaving our male and female cats at home in the care of our daughter. On our return we learned that Thomas, the un-neutered seventeen-month-old ginger tom, had gone missing. A week later we found him at an isolated house where two spayed cats live. We collected him, made a fuss of him and had him castrated. But eight days later he walked out of the door and has not been seen since. It is now five weeks since he disappeared and despite heroic efforts on my part, his fate remains a mystery. Have you any thoughts on the matter?

E.Y., Midhurst, West Sussex

Don't give up hope and keep searching. Ring all vets and rescue centres in a fifty-mile radius, sending a photo if possible. Contact local newspapers and radio about him. Put notices in community centres, newsagents, churches (with the vicar's permission), supermarkets, on lampposts, etc. Offer a small reward if you can. Check sheds, allotment buildings, barns, building sites (in case a cat is down among the floorboards or walled up by mistake), garages, attics, culverts – anywhere where a cat might get itself stuck.

Un-neutered tom cats are far more likely to roam than neutered ones and you left neutering late. It takes two or three months for the male hormones (and therefore male behaviour) to disappear after castration. If you find him, Thomas may become more of a homebody in future, but think about having him microchipped or using one of the new safe identification collars.

Long Lost Returning

Six months ago my daughter moved to be near us with her family and three cats. Her new house was about ten miles away from her old home. Three weeks later she and her family went on holiday leaving us to tend the animals. From the first day we never saw the youngest cat, despite asking around, calling, even going back to their previous home. Then, nearly fourteen weeks later, Socks walked in, thinner, muddy and with moth-eaten ears. He ate two tins of cat food and almost a pint of milk before going to sleep on the settee between the two children. He mewed nearly all night, he was so pleased to be home. He ate a great deal but has been out of the house very little since he returned home. Is this a record?

S.W., Brentwood, Essex

This isn't a record, though it's a good example of how cats do return sometimes after weeks. One cat survived forty-five days under floorboards. Another cat lost in Cornwall (while on holiday there with its human family) turned up six months later and, because posters were still around, was recognized and restored to its owners. Pipsqueak, a cat in Hereford, turned up three years after going missing!

Leaving by Train

My cat disappeared one wet and windy night. The next day I immediately inundated the area with notices on trees etc., and the first call I received was from a man saying he had seen a Siamese-shaped cat wearing a collar getting on to the last train to Richmond. My immediate reaction was that this was a hoax but I contacted the railway company and Richmond station, to no avail.

I continued to look in my area, had numerous phone calls, but was unable to find him. The first call preyed on my mind and I therefore contacted all the vets in Richmond and Kew. Two weeks after he had disappeared, I received a call from a lady in

Richmond who had seen a cat fitting his description sitting in her garden, which backed on to the railway line near Richmond station. On my second visit to her garden I called his name and he came immediately. I hope this story offers some hope to others whose cats may be missing.

A.J., Chiswick, West London

Other readers have also written in with stories of cats who have either returned home or been found after many months. Compote, an Abyssinian-type moggy, was adopted by her owners' daughter when they had to go to Korea, but went missing shortly afterwards. "Three-and-a-half years later my daughter was out collecting jumble for charity and in the garden of a house, about a quarter of a mile away, was Compote. The householder had been feeding her but was unable to have her in the house as she had rather a fierce dog." Sooty, a cat from Derbyshire, came home two-and-a-half years after going missing, while another missing cat, Bruno, was found years later "asleep on a very expensive eighteenth-century chair in the window of a local antique shop". It's a reminder for all of us, who lose cats, not to give up hope and to keep searching.

Strange Encounters

Several days ago I looked out of my window at 4.30 a.m. and noticed a fox in the neighbour's garden. Tabitha my large cat sat on the fence observing it. The fox jumped on to the fence about a foot away from Tabitha and for a few minutes they scrutinized one another. Then it jumped down into my garden and sniffed around, ignored by my other cat who was also in the garden. The cats are very frightened of dogs, yet showed no fear of the fox who surely was a potential predator. Could this be a common occurrence?

J.C., Rickmansworth, Hertfordshire

Foxes will not usually attack a full-grown healthy cat. Most fox–cat encounters show both animals either ignoring each other or displaying wary caution. Foxes will certainly attack a kitten or any cat which in some way can't fight back, but they are not going to risk cats' claws and teeth when they can more easily get a meal from dustbins or young rabbits. Adult cat bones have been found in foxes' stomachs but these may come from corpses found on the road or from cats wounded by traffic.

Tabitha seems to have a lack of caution about foxes. When she becomes elderly, or if she is ill, you would be well advised to make sure she stays indoors during the night.

We have two cats who are nervous of humans. Every night I feed the hedgehogs with cat food and on some nights we are also visited by a very large, healthy and fit fox. The cats show no fear of him and usually sit and watch him eat. Last night he picked up one of the ping–pong balls left lying around for the cats to play with and Eliza ran after him with all her fur and tail up to attack him. When the fox dropped the ball and continued to eat, she calmed down and just sat back to watch again. Was the cat wanting to play? It seems strange that the cats show no objection to him in the garden but, as soon as he touched one of their toys, attack him.

G.D., Enfield, Middlesex

If Eliza had her fur up I think she was trying to see him off, rather than play with him. The fact that she then just watched him suggests she wisely decided to play for time!

Our tabby also had a surprising time with a fox. It was late afternoon a few months ago when a fox appeared on our front lawn. At the same time Misty emerged from the front door and walked up the drive taking no notice of the fox. The fox looked mildly interested and then walked away. To our surprise our cat followed it down the garden and proceeded to show off, darting about in front of the fox which sat on a pile of logs watching! After a while it got bored and moved away. Is this normal behaviour or is our cat rather foolhardy?

C.F., Tonbridge, Kent

Perhaps your cat hasn't realized that foxes are potential enemies. Young or inexperienced cats sometimes take a bit of time to work out how to behave around foxes or even around other cats.

Just before it began to get dark my husband spotted Willy, our year-old Turkish van cross, walking in the paddock with a baby rabbit in his mouth. As he watched, a very large fox came out of the undergrowth just behind Willy and made straight for him. My husband shouted at it but it took no notice of him. Willy turned round, saw the fox and dropped his catch, which it picked up and made off with. Was the fox after the rabbit or was it really trying to take the cat?

A.B., Hastings, East Sussex

The fox was probably after the rabbit, rather than Willy. Its threatening behaviour worked and it got the rabbit without having to fight for it. In view of the fact there was a tin of cat food waiting for him at home, I think Willy showed good sense too!

Cats and Gardens
I would like to plead with cat owners not to wean their cats off the litter tray. I am repeatedly frustrated

in my attempts to grow flowers and vegetables by my neighbours' cats using all parts of my garden as their toilet area. Ultrasonic devices and high fences are not completely effective as a deterrent. In case it should be thought I am a cat hater, we kept a cat for eighteen years and she used a litter tray for the whole of her life. It can be done.

R.C., Doncaster, South Yorkshire

I agree that it is a mistake to wean a cat off a litter tray completely. If the cat is ill, or during Guy Fawkes' night, it will need to use a tray indoors anyway. Good cat owners should also make a toilet area in their own gardens, putting dry peat or sand under a hedge or under shrubs. By putting the contents of the litter tray there, it will encourage the cat to use the area, not the neighbour's seedbed. Occasionally, infuriated gardeners (not R.C. of Doncaster) throw missiles or even use air guns on intruding cats so it is safer for a cat to use its own garden. I think it is now time we had a cat owner code of conduct. Dog owners have to pick up their dog's poo from the pavement; we cat owners should try to encourage our cats to do their business on our territory, not somebody else's.

Indoor Cats

My two cats, an oriental short-haired female, Aye-sha, and a Siamese male, Hang Sen, stay indoors all the time. Do you have any ideas on the pros and cons of this situation? Mine have access to a large pen in the garden.

M.M., March, Cambridgeshire

Keeping two cats (not just one) indoors with an outdoor pen isn't cruel. It keeps them safe, saves neighbours' gardens from their mess, and spares the lives of wild birds and mice. But indoor cats need lots of games with their owners. Get a fishing-rod toy. Throw balls of paper or kitchen foil. In the wild a cat would hunt about ten mice a day, so aim at ten short games or thirty pounces every day.

Make sure your cats have plenty to look at in their

garden pen. Put a bird feeder up. Provide sitting places, preferably on ledges and shelves rather than the floor, at windows with the best view of passers-by, dogs, wildlife, and other cats. Provide scratching posts and perhaps a cat aerobic centre, which will give them a chance to climb.

Provide toys and change them daily. Christmas tree balls are easy to bat. Dangle thick ropes from a hook in the ceiling. Cardboard boxes with holes to get into. Newspapers to tear. Put dry food into puzzle feeders made of two yoghurt tubs glued together with holes punched in them. Hang these up. Bought toys include crinkle bags, fur-covered mice, etc.

Give food four times a day if possible. Or hide some of the food daily so your cats have to search for it – easiest with dry food. Finally, you can teach them tricks, as well as playing with them.

Christmas Tree

Phoebe, our indoor cat, adores the Christmas tree and won't leave it alone. Last year she had the whole thing down six times. She throws herself at it, climbs it, chews it and generally destroys it.

She's not otherwise a destructive cat, though she used to tear up my yucca plant when she was a kitten. I've tried putting orange peel or silver foil at the bottom of the tree to no effect. I tried spraying her with water but she just enjoyed that! What can I do?

P.M., Coulsdon, Surrey

Phoebe may have learned this behaviour on the yucca plant and it's going to be difficult to stop her doing it. "You will have to teach her not to do this, first with a piece of tinsel, then a bauble, and then a sprig of tree, before introducing her to the whole tree," advises David Appleby, a cat behaviour counsellor. "Try putting a scent she dislikes on these – eucalyptus oil, olbas oil or tea tree oil."

Unfortunately some cats start sniffing and enjoying these oils and if Phoebe is one of them, you will have to try something else. "Throwing a small bean bag to land just near her, when she starts playing with them, might do the trick," says David Appleby. "The danger in training cats in this way is that they may get too stressed, and then start spraying the tree. So if Phoebe looks as if she is getting frightened, stop immediately. It is infinitely better to have a battered tree than a spraying cat!"

Boisterous behaviour like this is more common with cats who don't have enough to do. You should make sure that Phoebe has her hunting needs fulfilled over Christmas, particularly if you see her stalking the tree! Play games with fishing-rod toys and pieces of string with her. You can also make her a food-dispensing toy by making holes in an empty plastic bottle and putting dried food in it.

Cats Leaving Home

I am desperate to find a solution to my four cats' difficulties. Two years ago Pepsi, the mother, had three kittens. She was a brilliant mother and I decided to keep all four. After weaning I had all four spayed and neutered but from that time onwards Pepsi turned against her offspring, growling and spitting. She doesn't come back to the house now, unless I fetch her. She spends most of her time in other houses. I do not wish to lose her and I should be grateful for any suggestions.

A.K., Manchester

Pepsi's behaviour is a variation of a natural instinct. "When cats live in the wild, the mother often turns on her offspring, pushing them out to find their own territory.

It's a way of making sure they do not compete with her for food," explains Vicky Halls, a cat behaviour counsellor. "The only slender chance of getting them all acclimatized is to treat her like a new cat."

Hire or borrow a kittening pen and put Pepsi in it with a bed, litter tray and food bowl. Feed the other cats near the pen. Move the pen from room to room, to give them the message that she has the right to be in every room. Only let her out of the pen when the others are not in the room. Make sure you cuddle her so that she smells of you. Continue this for at least a week, maybe two, until she has stopped hissing.

"Introducing a new cat in this way usually works well," says Vicky Halls, "but it isn't always effective with cats that already don't get on together. Sometimes they associate confinement with the other's presence, further destroying any chance of a better relationship. If Pepsi disliked the situation so much that she left home, she may just move out again once she is free to do so." If this happens, it will be kinder to find her a home where she can be a single cat.

Seeking Out His Old Home

I have four cats (one female and three neutered males). We moved house last October and I kept them all indoors for a week. When I let them out they all came back indoors and seemed completely settled into their new home. However, after about five months, one of the males, Ginger, decided to return to the old house which is about a mile away. Our old neighbour brought him back and Ginger seemed pleased to see us. Nevertheless he has kept on going back and I have to collect him nearly every day, which is a nuisance. He is not being fed because I left him once for four days and he was starving. He just won't return of his own accord. What can I do?

L.H., Stoke Gifford, South Gloucestershire

Most cats are instinctively attached to their territory and, because you have moved only a mile away, Ginger has found a way to get back to his. Now you have to make his old territory unattractive and his new territory attractive.

"Start afresh to reconcile him to his new home by keeping him indoors for five weeks," advises Emma Magnus, a cat behaviour counsellor. *"Use Feliway spray from your vet within the house to increase his feeling of security during this time."*

She recommends feeding several small meals a day, so that Ginger has to keep coming back to feed. You will also need to go round the old neighbourhood and ask people to shoo him away from his old haunts. The aim is to make his old territory so unpleasant that he will stay in the new.

Drug Sniffing, Substance Use and Cats Getting High

It's a shocking fact that many of our domestic cats are drug users. Like junkies they search out certain substances, sniff them, and then lie around behaving in a spaced-out fashion – meowing, foolishly rolling on their backs, rubbing their chins against things and generally getting high. Oddly enough their owners seem to find this funny. Respectable men and women who would be frantic if they saw their teenage children behaving in a similar fashion are completely laid back when it comes to their moggies. Reputable pet shops sell catnip sprays or dried catnip, for instance, and owners visit these dealers to buy substances to help their felines get high. About four or five out of every ten cats are susceptible to catnip, *Nepeta cataria*. Their genetic make-up means they can break down its active component, nepetalactone. Their reactions are more like those of a pot smoker than a drinker. Catnip doesn't make them fighting drunk; if anything, it makes them spaced out. They will rub their chins against it, lick it, sometimes dig it, and eat it if possible. Then they lie about behaving in a rather silly way, making inappropriate gestures and noises.

Some people have argued that the smell of catnip is similar to the scent of a female cat on heat. It is true that cats on catnip use some of the same gestures as female cats on heat – but only some, not all, of the gestures. So we cannot assume moggies on catnip are in some kind of sexual frenzy. Catnip moreover is appreciated by both sexes, neutered and entire, and if you plant it in your garden you may find cats from miles around coming to visit you. But doting owners who buy the garden version of this plant, catmint or *Nepeta faassenii*, may find it doesn't give their pussycats a fix. A few cats will get off on this cultivated variety of catnip but most won't. Other plants which seem to have a druggy effect are valerian (the herb *Valeriana officinalis*, not the fleshy *Centranthus ruber* that lives on walls), the climbing kolomite vine, *Actinidia kolomikta*, and inside the home the potted spider plant, *Chlorophytum comosum* "Vittatum".

John Foster, a vet who is researching this rather obscure byway of feline behaviour, has found very little written about cat drug taking! However, reports from *Telegraph* readers led him to comment: "A startling finding is the number of cats that seem to be able to get their fix by rubbing at the plant, seemingly not doing much with it, or even sitting beneath it or in it and getting the same results."

Smells are certainly more important to cats than to humans. They have an extra nasal organ no longer found in human beings: the vomeronasal organ within their noses which they use to assess their food. "Within a few moments of sniffing at the odours coming from the food the cat has a profile of the amino acids in the proteins on the plate," says John Foster. It is probably this extra sense that allows them to absorb the plant odours. Human junkies have to eat, smoke or sniff their drugs up their nose into the nasal cavities. Cats can absorb the psychoactive ingredients at a relative distance.

Should we encourage them to do this? Frankly it doesn't seem to do much harm. Most cats presented with a catnip-scented object will spend up to twenty minutes rubbing on it or licking it, and after a period of silly behaviour will just leave it alone. Unlike humans, they seem to know when they have had enough. But we should probably be careful about enabling our feline loved ones to get high too often. "It is unwise to put it on food," says John Foster. "It might over-stimulate the nervous system." Besides, not only do cats get bored with catnip toys if they are just left lying around, but the catnip scent fades. Keep the toys in a box or bag with some dried catnip to keep the scent strong, and take them out for brief periods of play.

It's also probably worth checking up on your cat, if you find it taking an unhealthy interest in garden plants. Some, like foxgloves for instance, are poisonous or, like pampas grass, dangerously sharp to eat. Since you cannot train your cat not to eat a plant, dangerous ones should be banned from the garden. There are also poisonous or dangerous house plants.

But it's not just plants that turn cats on. You may find your moggy sniffing out objects like valerian herbal teas. Or hanging around near the cupboard under the sink in search of cleaning fluids and polishes. Some pussycats raid the dressing table or the bathroom for cosmetics or soaps. Others take an extraordinary interest in the contents of the fruit bowl. Pears seem to turn cats on, though the variety differs from cat to cat. The active ingredient may be amyl acetate, which would explain why several cats get a high from newly developed photographs. On the other hand some cats hate the smell of nail varnish, a much stronger form of the same chemical.

Finally, there are the cats that are turned on by their owner's body odour. They swoon with pleasure after sniffing armpits, or spirit away bits of dirty underwear to knead or sniff. Sniffing in this way probably helps them bond with us humans. A kitten has to smell its mother in order to find her nipple and to suckle her milk. Kittens with no sense of smell (either because researchers have removed it or because cat flu has impaired it) are almost unable to suckle. The younger the cat, the more likely it is to be interested in its humans' body odours. "Young cats often do a major sniff at the armpits and some get very excited about an owner's odours," says John Foster. "They don't necessarily stay interested in later life. They've got the imprint and so don't need to do it again."

Crazy about Lilac

I have two cats, three-year-old sisters Gus and Mungo, who eat plants. They both are crazy about a miniature lilac I bought last year by post from a *Telegraph* advertisement. The one lilac has grown well but the other, labelled as *Syringa villosa*, is struggling to live because they rub it, lean against it, sniff it and lick it. I haven't seen them eat it, but they have broken the lower branches and pulled off leaves. I have now dug it up and put it in a pot and placed it in the greenhouse. After "loving" it they are very dozy and happy but show no other ill effects. The second plant that Gus eats is an ornamental grass. I can't find its botanical name except for *Glyceria maxima* 'Variegata'. I have enclosed a piece of it (together with the leaf from the *Syringa villosa*). Gus loves actually eating this grass and does so whenever she remembers it, especially if I use it indoors in a flower arrangement! She has no apparent ill effects and once started, eats it to the base.

E.D., Chipping Sodbury, South Gloucestershire

Matabi

My first attempt to grow *Actinidia kolomikta* was foiled within twenty-four hours of planting. Not attributing it to anything other than an unfortunate outbreak of feline warfare in the flower bed I promptly replaced it. This was also savaged, despite having been surrounded with a positively Fort Knox-like fortification of wire netting for its protection. By an extraordinary coincidence I was reading an old magazine in the vet's waiting room and came across an article on the plant matabi, *Actinidia polygama,* which has been scientifically established to have much the same effect on some cats as *Nepeta cataria* . . . Apparently the chemical concerned is actinidine, which is structurally similar to the nepetalactone found in catnip. Having bravely put out yet another shoot from its mangled remains this year, my plant is still struggling to survive – and although the cats seem temporarily to have lost interest in it, the wall covering of pink-and-white variegated leaves for which I had hoped still seems a very long way off.

J.W., Burnham-on-Crouch, Essex

Rip Van Winkle Daffs

The writer who had a choice *Actinidia kolomikta* destroyed by her cats has my sympathy. I had a healthy, thriving fourteen-inch high *Actnidia chinensis,* or Chinese gooseberry, that completely disappeared overnight. Close inspection revealed bite-size pieces, chewed and discarded, all round the planting area. I try to restrict their garden snacking to the catmint, but one of my little darlings has a springtime habit of biting off the heads of my miniature daffodils (variety 'Rip Van Winkle').

C.S., Maidstone, Kent

Foxgloves in the Spring

We have two cats, litter brothers. When younger the ginger one would chew cactus but this stopped as he got older – we think he might have been teething! He doesn't do it now but does occasionally bite on rose twigs and others with spines. His brother, black with slight oriental tendencies, loves foxgloves but only when they are young and just coming through. He rubs all over them, chews and kicks at them (of course, they're the unusual ones) in the spring. As they get bigger, he loses interest. Neither of them go mad for catnip. They are both partial to the ornamental grass which is tall and thickish with green–striped leaves.

J.R., Romford, Essex

Neapolitan Cyclamens
I have a neutered tom about four years old who has a strange fascination for Neapolitan cyclamens. Two small plants are normally on my windowsill where Sambo often sits. Latterly he has taken to eating the young leaves ravenously. I moved them into my bedroom, a room that has always been out of bounds to him, and where there is a much higher windowsill, and he has shown no wish to enter.

I was in there the very next morning, door ajar, when Sambo hurried in, jumped on to my stool, then the dressing table and up to the windowsill where he started consuming the leaves again. He did not see me put them there and he could not see them from outside the room. Therefore he must have smelled them as he hurried to get to them with such determination.

M.J., Foston, Derbyshire

Bog Bean Lover
We have three small ponds in the garden and in spring our cat, Hillary, chews the new shoots of the bog beans, *Menyanthes trifoliata*. We have seen other

107

cats passing through the garden doing the same thing, so that plant must have something in it that appeals to them. They don't bother with it any other time of year, and show no interest in the flowers, so whatever turns them on must just be in the fresh shoots.

M.G., Nuneaton, Warwickshire

In Love with Valerian

Our three-year-old female tabby's amorous propensities are excited by the outside wrappers of certain herbal teas, which among their ingredients contain valerian. Tabitha's reaction is such that we haven't risked the whole tea bag. Even our seventeen-year-old black-and-white female, Tilly, shows immoderate excitement. This reaction to valerian is known, but the low concentration likely to be present on the wrapper may be of interest. A similar reaction is produced by Flash liquid floor cleaner – the mop head is subjected to intense bouts of rubbing and licking.

R.W., Newnham, Kent

Chewing Artichokes

Our cat, Demi (short for Demetra), has developed an odd habit. We live in Cyprus and at the end of our garden we have thirty artichoke plants. Demi spends ages chewing the leaves and stalks. It is the only plant in our garden to which she pays any attention.

D.N., Paphos, Cyprus

Dangers of Pampas

I had a dear little cat, Leonie, a tiny tortoiseshell. When she was three years old she suddenly went off her food. One day I noticed something protruding from her nostril which she would not let me touch. I took her straight to the vet who said it was a piece of pampas grass. I left her for him to anaesthetize and extract it, which he did, but the little thing died under the anaesthetic. She must have been worn out with pain. The grass was about six inches long and had been lodged in her head for a month, completely undetectable until it began to work its way out. Pampas grass is viciously sharp loathsome stuff which she couldn't chew. I wish it could be banned.

H.M., South London

Florist Carnations

One of my spayed tortoiseshells finds florist-supplied carnations irresistible. Strangely, garden-grown pinks do not have the same appeal. She will sit and lick carnations (flowers themselves, for preference, though stems and leaves too on occasion) endlessly in the same way as she will also lick human skin, mine particularly. She is very partial to bath-foam-covered limbs and will perch on the side of the bath licking away until the limb is removed in irritation. I have always assumed that this cat as mildly deranged as her sister shows no such tendencies.

C.B., Camberley, Surrey

Amaryllis in the Shade

I recently adopted a year-old black-and-cream tabby female who fell in love with my amaryllis plant. She stroked the leaves, smelled the flowers and was fascinated by the stamens. Eventually she broke off the one remaining flower. I put it in water and it was her favourite plaything. She was very gentle and she left no visible traces of her interest in the flower. As it faded her interest waned. I thought perhaps the colour had attracted her and replaced it with a geranium but after a few perfunctory sniffs she lost interest in the scent and was only mildly interested in the petals. She looked really beautiful when she was splaying the amaryllis – her black-and-cream coat, the scarlet flower and the shining glass and most of all, her look of intense concentration.

Her favourite toy is a small round Indian fan made out of stiff paper with a wooden handle, painted on one side with a bird and on the other with flowers. She prefers the side with the bird. She bites it, licks it and drags it about and the paper makes a most satisfying crackle.

D.H., Slough, Berkshire

Lametta Tinsel

Our cat, Tigger, is not addicted to any of the plants described in your column, but he loves Lametta tinsel. We haven't bought any for years but he always finds little bits still left in the box of Christmas decorations. He won't touch ordinary tinsel, only the Lametta.

J.B., Wokingham, Berkshire

Emery Boards

I wonder if you might know what cats like about emery boards. Jeffrey, the Tonkinese, steals them but the others, my two oriental short-haired females and my half-Havana male, are always attracted when my daughter and I are using emery boards. I also had a cat who was strongly attracted by the smell of Blistereze.

M.M., March, Cambridgeshire

My cat gets very excited if I file my nails with an emery board when she is nearby. I presume it is the smell which interests her, but she tries to grab the file, smells it and puts it in her mouth. I have also found emery boards left on the table with teeth marks in them. I assumed this was a personal quirk to Bagheera until I mentioned it to a cat owner at work who went home and tried filing her nails while her cat was on her lap. The same excitement was generated.

J.W-E., Aberdeen

Deep Heat Sniffer
My cat, Petal, finds the smell of Deep Heat very exciting and will enjoy a good lick if she can. The last time Petal managed it, she started chasing her tail like a kitten. I really felt she was stoned. She also finds Vick very exciting. I find this extraordinary, as with cats' sensitive noses I would expect them to find the smell thoroughly unpleasant.

E.L., Cardiff

Skink and Colgate Toothpaste
We changed from using toothpaste in a squeezy tube to the vertical type of tube (same brand of toothpaste: Colgate Regular Flavour). Since then Skink, our cat, has insisted in putting his head in our mouths at every bedtime to smell our teeth, even on one occasion licking my husband's back teeth. He shows no interest in the toothpaste while still in the tube. Yes, we know this isn't a very hygienic habit.

P.A., Carterton, Oxfordshire

A Passion for Deodorant
Jumpers, our seventeen-year-old tortoiseshell cat, has developed a passion for my roll-on deodorant, doesn't matter which make. She makes a thorough nuisance of herself while I'm getting up until I put it down on the floor, whereupon she nuzzles it wildly. We estimate this behaviour started about four years

ago. It might have coincided with the death of her sister, Quince. Or does the deodorant contain some enzyme or pheromone missing in her old age?

H.N., Hebden Bridge, West Yorkshire

What a Lovely Pair

I have a problem with my two tortoiseshell cats, spayed sisters aged eight. They have an on-going love affair with a bowl of pears! I bring the fruit home, wash it and put it in a bowl of mixed fruit, but it is the pears that have this fatal attraction. Can you suggest why this particular fruit should cause such a flutter? The pears are licked, purred over and rolled on.

J.M., Croydon, Surrey

When I read that other cats attack pears, it was like learning you are not the only one with a rare disease! Topaz, our white female, can render a bowl of pears uneatable in minutes. She also mauls Cox's orange pippins and now we have to hide these fruits. The pears we have are mostly Conference.

S.P., Tenterden, Kent

Our cat, Smaug, a neutered ginger tom, loves Conference pears. He chews them and runs his mouth corner along the stalk. He likes grapes (generally White Cape grapes) and is obsessively affected by the smells of Domestos (no other bleach will do!) and Dettol for which he will kill and on either he gets as high as a kite. Now when it comes to food his range includes chocolate (flake is favourite), poppadums, cheddar and grated Parmesan, All Bran bite size, Marmite (can you believe it?), smoked turkey or smoked mackerel or smoked salmon, probably anything smoked, Philadelphia cheese, Flora margarine, etc., etc. Additionally, and not very hygienically, he will defend the chopping board against all comers when we are preparing any root vegetables and cabbage!

V.H., Kington Magna, Dorset

One of my two spayed sibling brother cats, Whizzer and Chips, aged fourteen, is in love with . . . bananas! Green seedless grapes and pears come close runners-up but then Chips is a trifle fickle. The fruit bowl usually ends up on top of the highest kitchen cabinet or under cover of an old-fashioned food net. And yes, they are not only licked, purred over and rolled on, but dribbled over too. All fruit in this house has to be washed several times over before human consumption. As to cause, I have always wondered whether it is to do with the chemicals used in crop spraying of these particular fruits, as opposed to natural alkaloids within the plants. Catnip has always also been the number one favourite "high". We have tried growing our own, but alas the young plants don't stand a chance, as they are flattened or licked to death each spring not only by our boys but by any visiting neighbourhood cats.

P.L., Bournemouth, Dorset

We are the proud owners of Sophie, a seal point kitten. This week, having been struck down by a tummy bug and feeling frail, all I wanted to eat was a tinned pear. Sophie practically climbed into the bowl and shared the pear with me. Mind you, she does like broccoli and hot cross buns.

E.C., Craven Arms, Shropshire

My cat goes into a frenzy with pears that I have left on a windowsill to ripen, biting them, rolling on them and finally knocking them on to the floor where he attacks them all over again. Conference pears definitely affect him most. He does, however, hate the smell of my nail varnish and shoots off my lap if I start painting my nails.

J.C., Standlake, Oxfordshire

Just recently we noticed Chloe, one of our four cats, rubbing herself over the pears in our fruit bowl. We couldn't understand why she was doing this, especially as none of the others seemed interested. The pears in question were a variety called Rocha. She doesn't seem at all interested in Conference pears.

J.H., Horsham, West Sussex

Fresh Photographs
One of my Siamese cats is drawn to photographs. If left lying around he will lick and chew them and gets cross when stopped. He will even try to open the enclosing envelope to get at them.

M.H., Halesowen, West Midlands

Olives
Our ancient stately mog Ethel, a spayed tortoiseshell, goes into ecstasy over olives. First she sniffs, licks and crushes the olives with bouts of head rolling, and finally she chomps them up, not forgetting to lap up the brine left in the dish. Black or green olives are equally popular but her favourites are those olives stuffed with anchovies. Not so daft. I hasten to add that here in southern Spain most floors are tiled or made of marble – hence no carpets to worry about.

A.D., Cadiz, Spain

My cat Boris, a short-haired British blue, appears to find pickled olives, particularly green ones and those

114

stuffed with pimentos, irresistible. He repeatedly rubs his chin and face over the olive and drools copiously. Although he doesn't actually eat it, he goes into a purring fit of ecstasy until the olive is dry. He has done this ever since he was a kitten.

R.T., Saffron Walden, Essex

Rubbing Vick

Our late, very lamented ginger tom, Clyde, changed from a placid gentle softie to a clawing dervish when he smelled either the chest-rub ointment Vick or the liquid Vapex. I use both of these when I have a cold and the only way to stop him licking and clawing me when I used either of them was to put a little on a separate corner of the duvet. In the end we shut him downstairs when we had colds. Clyde did chew catmint but it did not have the same effect on him and he wasn't so interested in it.

J.L., Framlingham, Suffolk

Olbas Oil

I'm the proud owner of a rather spoiled moggy who is addicted to olbas oil. She can smell it at a great distance. If you have it on a tissue in a pocket or even up a sleeve, she will chew her way through the garment until she gets at it. She happily spends hours with a tissue which has the oil on it.

N.I., Watford, Hertfordshire

Wet Swimwear

My exotic shorthair cat adores the smell of swim-wear on our return from the pool. She will pull garments from the towel rail and roll ecstatically in them. I do not know if this smell contains amyl acetate or if she is responding to a different aroma. Interesting, anyway.

J.T., Bingley, West Yorkshire

Mortimer's Fix

Mortimer, our nine-year-old tabby, has one way of getting his fix. Immediately he hears anyone open the study bedroom door, he rushes to get in there. He jumps on the bed and knocks off a shelf a small wooden vase which he then holds between his paws and licks the bottom of. If he loses it down the side of the bed he will then lick the shelf until it is quite wet. Although the vase is polished, it is the unpolished bottom that he licks. The shelf is veneered contiboard. No other wooden object seems to attract him.

P.W., Hindhead, Surrey

Roll-up Cigarettes

My late-departed cat, Bob Dylan Marlais Thomas Clarke-Chilton, or Dylan for short, was an ardent dried catnip sniffer. I once planted a bought catnip and within ten minutes I found Dylan sitting before the now bald stems with a look of heaven-found in his eyes, and a lot of leaves in his stomach. His other favourites were olbas oil, Crest toothpaste, and Marmite – which used to make his eyes water and nose screw up but he never stopped licking or sniffing. Finally, we had a friend over who made a roll-up cigarette. Dylan went wild for the tobacco and the smell on our friend's fingers afterwards. But we often wondered, as the chap had flown in from Holland, whether it was pure tobacco or some other substance.

P.C., Skipton, North Yorkshire

Foot Fixation
Lady, my fourteen-year-old tortoiseshell-and-white, has an alarming fixation with my feet. No matter what condition they are in she will lick, bite and chew them. She will lie on her back and grab them and go to sleep or just rub up against them. What I find strange is that she will do this if I have just come in from shopping with hot sweaty feet; when I have socks or stockings on or even shoes or slippers; when I have just stepped out of the bath and talcumed them or rubbed moisturizer in them. Nobody else's feet will do! She doesn't want to know about my husband's or daughters' feet. Can John Foster tell me if my feet could be giving off amyl acetate, like the pears or snapshots sniffed by other cats?

A.H., West Wickham, Kent

Wet Hair
My daughter and I are the proud owners of a five-year-old female tabby, who has the unusual habit of eating wet hair. My daughter's freshly shampooed hair is an obsession with Rikki, who walks into, nudges and eats Lynn's thick curly wet hair.

A.D., Reading, Berkshire

Balding Cats, Furballs, Feline Coiffure, and Fleas

Balding or thinning hair, greying or fading hair, tangles and dirt are what worry us cat owners, both in ourselves and in our feline loved ones. Only we don't take our cats to the hairdresser – we are their hairdressers! And there is no great cosmetic industry selling feline dyes, hair oils or conditioners – yet.

All cats should be brushed once a week. This helps us owners to bond with our cats and allows us to spot any skin troubles, abscesses from cat fights or segments of tapeworm, those white rice-like bits which wiggle so disgustingly near the feline bottom! Elderly cats and fat cats who can't groom themselves properly need extra grooming, while long-haired cats need brushing every day if possible to prevent knots and mats forming in their coats. If these are not removed by brushing or cutting out with scissors, they eventually make the skin underneath inflamed and even raw. Neglected long-haired cats can get so badly knotted and sore that they need to be anaesthetized while their hair is cut away.

About once a month I get a desperate letter from an owner whose cat is going bald. For some reason the animal has started to over-groom itself, licking so hard that it exposes a bald patch of inflamed skin. Occasionally the cat can be seen literally tearing its hair out in tufts.

The most common cause of this is simply fleas. Somehow the cat has developed an allergy to the saliva in flea bites and just one bite is enough to set up severe itching. And, of course, the cat scratches where it itches. Yet we owners often won't believe that fleas can be the problem. We don't like to think that there has been a third party – a flea or even hundreds of them – in our close relationship with our cats. Those of us who share the bed with our pussycats like to think that they are flea free. Our vets tell us there must be fleas, but we don't see any fleas and believe that therefore there are none. The name of this game is denial – the refusal to admit an unpleasant fact! Some vets, failing to find any fleas in the fur, go along with our denial. Yet about one in three domestic cats, even the much-loved and pampered animal, has fleas.

Even when owners accept that the cause is flea allergy, they will often just treat the cat with products from the pet shop – collars or sprays for the fur. Sometimes they forget to treat other animals in the home, and they almost always forget to treat the house itself. At first the cat seems a little better. After a few weeks, the fleas come back and the cat starts scratching again. Since most people have no idea about how to banish fleas successfully, they are under the illusion that there must be another cause.

If flea treatment seems not to be working, the vet helpfully gives the cat an injection of either steroids or female hormone. This reduces the inflammation and the cat stops scratching. The fur begins to grow back. But often the fleas are still flourishing in the house, if not on the cat, and when the injection wears off the inflammation appears again. For it takes only a single flea bite to start up the allergy. Only if fleas are completely eradicated, can the merry-go-round of vet's visits cease.

Ordinary insecticide sprays and collars etc. will not get rid of fleas altogether. Fleas start life as eggs, then hatch into larvae scuttling around the dark areas in the house, eating skin dander and any organic rubbish. They then change into pupae, finally emerging as the adult flea, which waits to jump on to any moving objects. The flea bites the animals and then lays its eggs, and the cycle starts up again. If you spray your pet with ordinary insecticide sprays, these kill the adult fleas but leave the eggs, the larvae and pupae of the flea population unharmed. These hatch out and fleas arrive again. But now there are products which interfere with this life cycle. To check for fleas, brush the animal over a piece of white damp paper. You won't see little beasties. But you may see small dots of "dust" which slowly ooze a brownish colour into the damp paper. These are flea dirts. Even if you can't see anything, the pet might still have fleas. Sometimes you can feel little seed-like bumps on the skin – this is a reaction to fleas.

Occasionally cats suffer from what is called atopy, a generalized hypersensitivity, not linked with flea allergy. To reduce the symptoms, vets often use steroids. These are usually given either as pills on a one day on, one day off basis, or by injection every two months or so. Because these drugs have side effects, the body has to be given some drug-free time even though the skin irritation is likely to return during these periods.

There are a very small number of cats who have food allergies too. They often have lesions round the face and mouth. Get your vet to prescribe a special diet and stick to it.

Stress occasionally causes a cat to over-groom and oriental breeds are more susceptible than moggies. Identifying the stress is not easy; it will need careful observation. Possible stresses include bullying by other cats, change of routine, boredom, or pain of some kind. Pain can also lead a cat literally to tear its hair out. Teeth troubles in particular can produce this reaction. So get your vet to give an all-over health check including teeth.

Hair Care

I have a long-haired white Persian cat, Sasha. Despite occasional brushing, her hair develops into knots which are almost impossible to remove. Is there anything I can do to prevent this happening?

G.M., Burghfield Common, Berkshire

The knots are forming because you are brushing only occasionally. Long-haired cats need brushing all over for at least five minutes every day. I tackle my long-haired cat with a slicker brush, or a narrow metal comb, or both if I am feeling conscientious. Then I go over again with a bristle brush.

If I miss two days or more, mats develop quickly. For these I use a pair of sharp nail scissors, and cut away at the mats little by little. The grooming time is a bore, but sores will develop underneath bad mats and a severely matted cat may even have to be anaesthetized by the vet before the mats can be cut away. I also clip short the fur round my cat's bottom, to prevent mess. If your cat dislikes being brushed, use food treats as a reward while brushing.

Brushing the Bottom

Our long-haired female cat, formerly a stray, gets mess caught on the hair round her bottom and when I try to clean her she is very bad tempered. She isn't very good about brushing and I frequently have to cut knots from her coat. Can you please advise me what to do?

H.A., Wigston Magna, Leicestershire

Long-haired cats need daily brushing to prevent knots and the easiest way to train them is to start when they are kittens, something you can't do with a rescue cat. So lay in a store of a really delicious treat like dried or fresh prawns. Holding the treat in the left hand, let the cat nibble it while you brush down the back. Only when the cat fully accepts this brushing, proceed to brushing the neck ruff.

The next step is to hold the treat at ground level so the cat has almost to lie down to reach it. Say "Lie down" while you do this. When the cat lies down, give the treat. When this response is established, hold the treat so that the cat has to lie on its side and brush a little along the side of the body before giving the treat. Next hold the treat in such a way that the cat has to lie on its back to nibble it. When it does this, reward it with the treat. Then brush round the tail a little, still holding the treat where the cat can nibble it, before giving it. Most cats will respond by moving their back

121

paws nearer the head, thus exposing their tail area. You can take off any mess with a metal comb.

You will need endless patience to make sure each stage is established before you proceed to the next one. It will take weeks, maybe months. If you haven't the time to do this, experiment with different foods to see if you can get a drier motion and get another person to hold the cat while you clip the hair short round her bottom every six weeks or so.

Static Electricity

Zubin, my six-year-old Siamese, likes nothing better than a game of rough and tumble with me, but every time I go to play with him I end up with an electric shock in my fingers. Is there anything I can do to prevent this?

R.M., Birdingbury, Warwickshire

The brush you use to groom him may encourage static electricity. Try using a slicker brush and metal comb instead. Put a little baby powder into his coat while grooming him, and then brush it out – in a room where you can easily vacuum up the powder afterwards!

Feline Moulting

Why does Mopsy, my five-year-old cat, moult all the year round? She also has a stary coat, but nevertheless a good appetite.

J.F., Brentwood, Essex

A cat living out of doors would shed its hair in early summer and grow thicker hair in autumn ready for the winter. "In our centrally heated houses, there's no need for a thick strong coat, so they just shed a little hair all the time," says Eric Wickham-Ruffle, an international cat judge of Persian and other cats. "For a cat of a dark warm colour with greasy hair, rub warm bran into the coat and brush out. For pale colour cats, rub in Johnson's baby talcum, and then brush it out thoroughly with a soft brush." It's important to brush out either the bran or the talc, otherwise your cat will eat it as she grooms herself.

There are now special products in pet shops to encourage glossy healthy hair in pets. These are usually a mixture of evening primrose oil, fish oil and vitamin E. Do not exceed the recommended dose.

Colour Change

My husband's cat, Edgar, is changing colour. We got him from the RSPCA a year ago where he was advertised as black and white. Now he is developing huge gingery shoulders that look even brighter in sunlight. Everyone is commenting on his chameleon-like transformation. Have you any ideas what is going on?

K.K., Sutton Coldfield, West Midlands

There isn't much research information about ageing hair colour changes in cats, perhaps because there's no market for feline hair dyes! Black cats get extra white hairs and sometimes tabbies develop darker stripes. "Some colour genes exist in kittens but do not show themselves till later life," says David Watson, a vet with an interest in hair colouring. "There are also colour changes associated with coat shedding, hormone changes, and day length." Sunlight sometimes makes visible the otherwise hidden markings on a cat – for instance, the underlying tabby stripes in the coat of a black cat. Skin disorders can also affect coat colour, so if you are in any doubt, take Edgar to a vet.

Skin Irritation

My silver tabby cat has been licking herself bald for ten months and is being treated with steroids by the vet. She also has herbal tablets and a drop of evening primrose oil daily. My vet agrees she is very difficult to treat, so I would be grateful for any suggestions.

J.C., Grouville, Jersey

Fleas or other parasites are the most common cause of cats licking themselves bald. "The cat may not have fleas on it, because it has licked so much that the evidence is removed," says David Grant, a vet with a special interest in dermatology. "It's often difficult for vets to persuade owners that fleas are the problem." So, even if you think your cat hasn't got fleas, get your vet to prescribe an effective flea treatment for use on the animal and treat your house (not the animal) with a spray containing methoprene. It will take several weeks before the fur starts growing back.

"Eight out of ten cat allergies are due to fleas, but there are also a few cats suffering from general hypersensitivity or very occasionally food allergies," says David Grant. "Veterinary dermatologists usually treat the skin irritation either with Prednisolone pills on alternate days or a long-acting injection every two months. These have fewer side effects than some of the other products." Cats will also sometimes pull out their own fur, because of stress, illness or pain.

Fur Pulling

When the severe hair loss round Flora's hindquarters began nine months ago she was seen by two vets, neither of whom found any sign of fleas. Both suspected a hormonal problem and prescribed Ovarid, Thyroxin and Orandrone, none of which had any effect. Eventually she was seen by a different vet and a close examination revealed a few bits of debris that could have been from fleas, though no actual fleas. This vet prescribed a spray and a monthly dose of Program for Flora and the dog. From that point on recovery was quite dramatic. It all seems to show that even a single flea is enough to trigger the allergy if your cat happens to be highly sensitive to them.

J.B., Godalming, Surrey

Pain Causing Hair Pulling

My ten-year-old black cat pulled out vast patches of fur. There were no fleas. Eventually the vet discovered a tumour on the side of his tongue. He could not clean himself properly because of the pain in his tongue so he tore out the fur in his distress. I would suggest other readers make sure they check out this possibility with the vet.

S.M., Ilminster, Somerset

Mouth pain, or indeed any kind of pain, can make a cat pull out its fur. It's always worth routinely treating for fleas, but also get the vet to check for anything that might be causing pain.

Lavender Oil
My cat Penny suffered repeatedly from flea allergy around the base of her tail. After trying various sprays and injections to no avail I found the answer, courtesy of a friend who was interested in aromatherapy. A couple of drops of lavender oil, either on my hand or her brush, stroked over the affected area has proved very effective and she has been free of the problem for over twelve months! Even my vet was impressed.

B.M., Poulton-le-Fylde, Lancashire

Hair Pulling and Stress
My Siamese, Saffis Chocoletti, is pulling out her fur especially on her back. She seems to over-groom, licking then pulling. The vet thought it might be flea allergy, but there is no sign of fleas or flea dirt on her. She is a much-loved cat but will pull even when sitting on our bed having been cuddled and played with. It is difficult to believe this is stress induced. How can I stop her?

L.B., St Albans, Hertfordshire

It's normal for a cat to groom itself after cuddling. Not only is it rearranging its coat, it is picking up your scent and reassuring itself about the relationship, says Sarah Heath, a vet and cat behaviour counsellor. "Excessive grooming and fur pulling can be a sign of stress." It's rather like humans biting their nails when nervous. Over-grooming is a response to stress, which can become a habit. "The stress could be a change in the home, visitors, tension among either cats in the home or cats in the neighbourhood, or not enough stimulation," says Sarah Heath. "If the fur pulling is very bad, the first thing to do is consult the vet. In some cases drug therapy or homoeopathic treatment may help but each case needs to be seen individually."

If you can identify the stress, then you can deal with it. A cat being bullied outdoors may need the cat flap closed, a bored indoor cat may need more stimulation. Cats who can't cope with other indoor cats, or with a change in the home, should be given a covered indoor pen, where they can get used to the changes or the presence of rivals. "They need to be given positive associations – by feeding or being given attention – while visitors are there," explains Sarah Heath. Working out what stresses a cat is easier with the help of a pet behaviour expert.

Flea Trap

I have recently seen advertised a plug-in flea trap, with sticky discs that attract fleas. Have you heard of it and if so do they work, please?

P.D., South Godstone, Surrey

These sticky flea traps probably do catch some fleas but they do not eradicate the flea population. In a house where the cat has fleas, there are flea eggs waiting to hatch, flea larvae waiting to pupate, pupae waiting to hatch, and then the adult fleas waiting to jump on the cat, bite, and lay eggs. A trap can have no effect at all on the eggs, larvae and pupae. If you want to eradicate fleas, get your vet to prescribe something for the cat, and spray the house with a spray which contains a flea growth inhibitor.

Worms

Titus, our neutered tomcat, is a real glorious tabby, weighing more than 14 lb. The problem comes when we need to worm him. He fights and spits and detects any form of medication and refuses his food. Most of the time we capitulate as he has to have such massive doses. How can he possibly have worms at that size?

M.A., Torpoint, Cornwall

At any weight cats can have worms – roundworms which they can pick up from the soil or from their prey, and tapeworms which come from fleas. In combined anti-worm

126

tablets, it is usually the anti-tapeworm drug which tastes unpleasant.

Simon Meyer, a vet, suggests that Titus could have an injection against tapeworms at the time of his vaccination. "For roundworms there are granules which are generally palatable or a pill which has a meat flavour. Ideally, Titus should be wormed every six months, so you should collect an extra dose of the granules or pill at vaccination time. If Titus has worms, they won't kill him. But tapeworms and possibly cat roundworms can occasionally infect humans."

Walking Dandruff

I have two long-haired cats aged six – extremely active with farmland and hillside to roam. Nigel and Sam have had fleas this summer and I've used a capsule on each and spray in the house. Now they have dandruff. I have always combed and brushed them. They are now on vitamin tablets prescribed by the vet. They won't take cod liver oil on their food (I'm having it holding my nose so as not to waste my money). I am about to try sardines in oil but they are not fish eaters. Have you any suggestions? It's like snow on a black field! (The dandruff I mean.)

I.H., Llangadfan, Montgomeryshire

Cats can suffer from something called "walking dandruff". "It is associated with parasites like Cheyletiella, a mite that lives in the fur," says vet David Godfrey. "The mite can also bite humans and you will see something like gnat bites often in a group of three. A vet should be able to see them with a microscope and prescribe something for them." Fleas can also cause dandruff so keep up the flea treatments. "Finally, overweight cats sometimes get dandruff along their backs. It may be because they can't groom themselves properly."

Old Age and the Last Goodbye

Old age wrecks both cats and humans. We lose our hair and teeth; so do cats. We sometimes get eccentric; so do cats. Unhappily some of us lose control of our bladders and bowels; so do cats. Yet a small percentage of us survive, to become centarians if we are humans, trentenarians in the case of cats.

Cats can outlive dogs by about a decade. The best-documented case of a long-living cat was a female tabby, Ma, who lived for thirty-four years, while another tabby, Puss, lived for a remarkable thirty-six years. There are cats reputed to have lived even longer, but there is no documentation to prove it and sometimes owners with lots of cats can be muddled about relative ages.

Cats living into their twenties, however, are no longer that rare. When I asked readers to tell me about elderly cats I heard of thirty-seven cats aged twenty years or over. The oldest living *Telegraph* cat was Tiddles, yet another tabby, who lived in rural surroundings. She had never been vaccinated and was still being put out at night because she refused to use a litter tray. Although a specially carpeted kennel was provided for her outside the back door, this tough golden oldie would refuse to use it!

"She is a bit wobbly on her legs, has lost both her figure and her purr, her coat is dreadful, otherwise she is bright-eyed, has all her teeth and has a very good appetite," wrote her owner. "She also bullies my other cat, a neutered tom, who is fourteen and lives in fear of the oldie."

Tiddles's age was rivalled by that of Basil, a black cat who had been put down only two weeks before my request for news of elderly cats. Basil had survived three changes of owner and four different types of skin cancer. The other outstanding *Tele-*

graph feline oldies were Mum who was twenty-six years old, Fluff, a twenty-five-year-old, and Molson who was same age. All were ordinary moggies, a couple of them originally strays, and three out of the five had never been vaccinated. All seemed to be cats of rather dominant character, rather like the human centenarians that I have met.

There were a further thirty-two cats who were aged twenty to twenty-four – all, except for two Burmese, a Siamese, and one Siamese cross, ordinary moggies. There seemed to be several who were strays or the offspring of farm cats, which would suggest they came from strong stock, with a genetic heritage of being able to survive in the wild. Most of them showed signs of arthritis, some were stone deaf, while Jinks had cataracts and Thomas was blind. Their owners coped with tenderness and the cats responded. Despite his blindness, Thomas still went caravanning and explored new territory while on his lead!

These old cats were surprisingly adaptable. Soda, a twenty-year-old, began to refuse to use the litter tray so her owner successfully taught her to go outside. Shelly, who had recently become an indoor cat, was learning to go for walks with a harness. Jemima, who lived with two other cats, adapted to country life after a move from London to Devon quicker than the other two younger felines.

Adaptable they may be, but older cats are not energetic. A small survey of middle-aged to elderly cats showed that they slept for twelve to eighteen hours a day. To get through these long hours of slumber, the cats would use human beds, places under or near a radiator (some in a cat hammock), cat beds, bean bags, clean clothes in the airing cupboard, sofas, armchairs, sunny spots in the conservatory, human laps, or places alongside boilers or Agas. They were expert in finding the warmest places in the house.

A preference for warmth may play a part in the way older cats quite often give up hunting in favour of the indoor life. And as their outside interests fell away, the survey showed that they turned to their owners for more companionship. Many demanded food several times a day, often refusing to eat unless their owners held their tail or provided some preliminary petting. Because they had lived with humans so long, they were expert at getting attention when needed.

Care and understanding of geriatric cats is growing, now that devoted owners are more likely to pay vets to help their cat survive well into old age. But even so, luck plays a part in feline survival. Vaccinations can protect against diseases like cat flu or leukaemia, but there are still no vaccines for Feline Immunodeficiency Virus or Feline Infectious Peritonitis. Cats in urban areas, where neighbourhood stray cats abound, run a greater risk of contracting diseases than those who live in the country. These illnesses have a devastating effect not only on the cats, but also on their owners. It is terrible to lose a cat, whatever its age. When a loved pet succumbs to illness after only a few years, owners are often almost inconsolable.

Part of my work as a pet agony aunt is comforting the bereaved. While our society recognizes the anguish felt by those who have lost a partner, a child or a parent, it is far less sympathetic to those who have lost a loved pet. People make crass remarks such as: "Why don't you get another one?" or "It was only an animal." A cat who has shared many years with its owner is not 'just an animal'. It is a member of the family. If its human owner lives alone, then the cat who shares her or his life, is more like a partner than a mere pet. The grief at its death can be overwhelming.

As with other forms of loss, grief is often accompanied by guilt and fury. Nowadays we expect vets to cure our animals and when they don't we can feel considerable anger. We also have unreasonable expectations of ourselves. Some bereaved owners torture themselves with the mistaken idea that they should somehow have protected their cat against incurable illnesses. I always hope that these unhappy owners will get another cat. Not as a replacement – no new cat will ever replace the much-loved cat who has died. For cats are proper personalities, richly individual in their behaviour and their responses. No, I hope that they will get another cat simply because there are so many cats desperately needing homes. Owners who grieve for their lost cat are the sort of loving people that other homeless or stray cats really need.

There is one comfort that I can offer the bereaved – my hope that, if there is a heaven, our cats will be there too. I look forward to meeting again white Moppet, black-and-white Fat Ada, gloriously tabby William and little dumpy black Mog. They are my friends and a heaven without friends simply wouldn't be heaven.

Golden Oldie

My darling Molson is nearly twenty-six years old. I found him when he was about a week old in Toronto, Canada. He was sitting in the sun. He is ginger. He spent six months in quarantine, has two teeth, is deaf, but still hanging in there. Every three months he goes to the vet, who says he is fine.

He sleeps a lot, loves his cuddles and I adore him. I am sure that he is alive today through all the loving he has received from me. He has been spoilt from the day I found him. When he was in quarantine I used to visit every day and sit in his cage and knit. People tell me I should put him down but I feel as long as the vet says he is OK and he is not suffering, then he has the right to live on. It brings tears to my eyes even to think about it. I don't think I am being cruel. After all the oldest recorded cat was thirty-six and that means Molson may outlive me yet.

F.K., Englefield Green, Surrey

Little Accidents

Cassie, my seventeen-year-old cat, is now leaving little deposits of both kinds near the front door during the day and the kitchen door where she is shut at night. She has a cat flap into the garden and litter trays, but she just squats alongside these. She's under the care of the vet for cystitis and thyroid problems, which are both under control. I have tried to erase lingering smells with disinfectant and carpet cleaner but she still returns to do it again.

M.G., Bath

Cassie is the equivalent of eighty years old or more and this may be the beginning of senile deterioration. Once cats have used an area as a toilet, the smell prompts them to repeat it there. You need to clear up using biological washing liquid, followed by surgical spirit. When it is dry, put down one of the special pet odour killers available from pet shops or vets' surgeries. Human products smell clean to us but sometimes smell of urine to cats.

"Shut the cat flap at night just in case there is something in the garden which frightens her. She shouldn't be out in the cold at her age anyway," says Vicky Halls, a cat behaviour counsellor. "Keep an eye on her cystitis – frequent squatting and blood in the urine may mean it has come back." She suggests giving Cassie a low litter tray, made from a human tray or a baking tray, placed on

top of newspaper. If she's arthritic, she can walk on to this, rather than make the effort to climb into a conventional litter box. Use small-granule litter and put some of her deposits there, so that it smells right. If there is still no improvement you may just have to confine her at night in a small area like a utility room with her litter and cat bed, where the accidents don't matter. Absorbent paper mats, sold to line litter trays but placed in strategic places, will help too.

Arthritic Cat

Sammy, my brown Burmese cat, is suffering from stiffness in his joints. He pulls at the fur on his front and back legs and I sometimes hear his bones snapping when he moves. But otherwise he is completely fit, apart from his kidneys not functioning perfectly. My vet says there is nothing available to help him but I am hoping that you might have some suggestions to alleviate his discomfort.

P.S., Ashford, Kent

Kidney disease in cats can affect the body's capacity to process drugs, which makes treatment difficult. "But there are painkillers which can be used short term for cats," says Caroline Prymak, a small animal surgical specialist who has a special interest in pain control. "If your vet agrees, you could give him these at times when he has overdone it and offer him some occasional relief." It is important to follow veterinary advice. Drugs that are safe for humans can poison cats. "The other possibility is to ask your vet about chondroprotective agents. These are safe to use long term and can give some pain relief, not immediately but after a few weeks." Your vet will have ruled out underlying skin disease as the cause of fur pulling, so it may be a response to the pain. But it is also worth treating him thoroughly for fleas, since sometimes fur pulling is caused by flea allergy. You can also make life easier for Sammy by making sure he doesn't have to make high jumps or cope with difficult obstacles during his daily routine. Control his diet so that he doesn't get overweight.

Yowling Cat

Our sixteen-year-old cat, Sam, has taken to howl-ing, very loudly! Originally he only did this in the garden, but now he does it indoors, even when sitting on his chair. Worst of all he now does it at night, and it is loud enough to wake you up – even with earplugs in! Cuddling him, stroking him or even shouting do not necessarily make him stop. Any ideas, please?

S.F., Fareham, Hampshire

First, get Sam checked out by the vet. "Sometimes cats with hyperthyroidism make this harsh noise," says Vicky Halls, a cat behaviour counsellor. Other symptoms of hyperthryoidism are weight loss and changes in behaviour. Occasionally the yowling occurs because the cat is deaf. If there is nothing wrong with Sam, then it may just be old age. Cats tend to "talk" more to their owners as they grow older, but this harsh yowling, unlike normal cat noises, seems to be a sign of senility. When Vicky Halls did a survey of older cats, she discovered quite a high proportion of night-time howlers. "As cats get older, they feel more insecure. They stop going out so much and turn more to their owner."

Putting Sam in a room far from the bedroom probably won't work because the howl is so penetrating. Yet if you get up and pet him each time he howls, he will only yowl the more. There's no easy cure, alas. "Putting the cat's bed in the bedroom might help Sam feel more secure," says Vicky Halls. "Of course, you might have to put the litter tray there too in case of accidents. With older cats, you just have to love them in their changing circumstances." Of course, Sam may be sleeping on your bed already!

Bereavement

Bradley, our elderly male cat aged sixteen, has recently been put down. Our other cat, a female, three-year-old Mollie, previously behaved very kittenishly, playing with a ball, pouncing, etc. This behaviour has changed almost overnight since Bradley has gone. She has adopted a slower walk and is not very interested in previous games. Is this the normal thing for a cat to do after losing an existing mate? We now have a new kitten, Susie, to replace our loss. Would this explain the behaviour?

M.R., Cambridge

I firmly believe that cats feel bereavement and loss. Worse still, they cannot always know why a loved companion has disappeared, which is why some vets recommend showing the dead body to the surviving pet. Occasionally, however, a surviving pet seems to enjoy being the sole focus of attention, once a companion has died. I believe Mollie could be mourning Bradley's departure. The other explanation is that she has become rather staid because of Susie. Kittens are always on the look out for games and Mollie may be behaving in a staid way because she doesn't want to be pestered!

Sympathy

Elsa, my silver-grey half-chinchilla cat, is very sweet and very gentle. On the morning of Diana Princess of Wales' funeral, she and my other cat, great creatures of habit, had breakfast and then I let them out into their fenced area of the garden, about the size of a tennis court. They came in dead on 12.30 p.m. for their snack lunch. On that morning I turned on the TV and sat down to watch. Just as the coffin was being carried into the abbey, to my surprise, Elsa came in. She put her front paws on my lap, a hitng she has never done before, then sat down beside me and never moved. When the coffin was being brought out, she got up and slowly left the room. I was very touched. I think she must have known I was sad, as lots of us were, and still are. Has anyone any ideas?

D.H., Alton, Hampshire

I am sure that she sensed your sadness. Although we are different species, cats and humans become expert in reading each other's feelings and meanings – from words, noises, and body language. Elsa's gentle sympathy, sitting near you throughout the funeral, moved me too.

Tumours

Sadly we had to have Sam, our cat, put to sleep last Friday at twelve years old, as he had tumours in his tummy and kidneys. He wasn't ill, didn't suffer at all, but we are devastated. However, I read in the *Telegraph* that the feline leukaemia injections had resulted in tumours in some cats in America. Sam had the jabs since 1993 when first introduced. I have been so worried about this.

C.S., Sutton, Surrey

In America a minute proportion of cats have developed vaccine-induced sarcoma in the scruff of the neck, the traditional site for vaccinations. It's been suggested that rabies vaccinations (routinely given there) or feline leukaemia vaccinations may be responsible. But vaccinations can have nothing to do with Sam's death, since his tumours were in a different area. Your loss is quite bad enough without your having to feel guilt.

"We really don't know enough about vaccines and cancer yet. The risk may come from adjuvants, things which are added to the vaccine, or the risks may be associated with any of the vaccinations," says vet David Godfrey. "It is still very important to have your cat vaccinated against feline leukaemia, since this is a killer disease."

Most vets in Britain have never seen a vaccine-induced sarcoma. But to be on the safe side, some owners have all vaccinations put into the hind leg of the cat, as low down as possible. In the worst possible scenario, if the cat develops cancer, it can then lose its leg rather than its life. Indoor cats will, of course, not need vaccinating against feline leukaemia since they do not meet other cats.

Feline Immunodeficiency Virus

Our cherished cat, Chico, eleven years old, died four months ago of Feline Immunodeficiency Virus. The vet said that, though she had been fully vaccinated, including against FeLV [Feline Leukaemia Virus], there is no vaccination against FIV and little hope of a cure for this disease which apparently resembles AIDS in humans. Please could you give us some information on how long the virus remains active, and what protective measures should be taken for the cat or kitten we are now planning to get? I really don't think we could face another death from this distressing disease. I should add that we intend to have our new pet tested for any dormant infection, but of course this affords no protection in the future. The neighbourhood is full of cats.

B.T., South-east London

Feline Immunodeficiency Virus is the feline equivalent of human HIV and lives in body fluids like blood and saliva. It's only necessary to wash and disinfect feeding bowls and litter tray, not the whole house. "Faeces in the garden will be washed away by rain or dried up by sun so a day or two should see them safe," says vet Simon Meyer. "The virus is remarkably easy to get rid of."

An FIV test is a good way to be sure your new kitten is not infected, as long as it is sixteen weeks or older. If you test a kitten before that age, it may show a false positive, because of the presence of antibodies from its mother.

The only utterly safe way to make sure your cat can never be infected is never to let it out of the house, but this can be a boring, even a miserable life for a cat if it is left on its own all day. Giving a cat freedom to go out of doors enriches its life but also brings risks. Only you can decide what you want to do. Incidentally, FIV cannot be caught by human beings.

Grief

The death of my beloved cat was shattering. The grief just won't go away. Whisky was only six years old. Had he been an elderly cat, perhaps I wouldn't feel quite so bad. It happened so quickly. When I got up in the morning he was in a terrible state. After various tests the vet confirmed he had the FIP [Feline Infectious Peritonitis] virus. They treated him for three weeks but to no avail and so he was put to sleep. I can't put into words how I feel. I loved him so much. He was my whole life. I keep asking myself – why my cat? I keep tormenting myself – why didn't I somehow know he had this terrible disease? Perhaps before it took hold, I could have had him treated. It's nearly three months now, but I still can't come to terms with it. I've shed a million tears, even as I am writing this letter. I miss him so much. I don't think the pain will ever go away.

D.M., Bristol

There is a piece of prose (a soppy one, I agree) which never fails to move me. I do not know its author but it goes like this:

'Just this side of heaven is the Rainbow Bridge, a haven for cats and other pets who have died. There our cats live in the warm sunshine, with their favourite foods. The countryside has long grass to explore, hedges to hunt in, and gardens where they can relax. Animals who were old and infirm become young and healthy again. They are as well and vigorous as we remember them from the old days.

"There is just one thing missing for their perfect happiness. For, though they enjoy their time in Rainbow country, they are waiting. Then the day dawns when an

individual cat suddenly stops. Its bright eyes look intent. Its tail goes upright. It knows something wonderful is about to happen. Hurriedly it leaves the others.

"For it has spotted you. There you are and it runs to meet you, tail bolt upright. The reunion is joyful. It rubs against your legs, purring just as it always did. Once more you see the animal whom you have always remembered and always missed.

"Then, together, you cross the Rainbow Bridge into heaven."

Appendix

Cat Experts

Steven Andrews is a qualified veterinary surgeon who, after spending five years working in small animal practice, joined Pedigree Masterfoods as a veterinary business consultant. He became Veterinary Marketing Manager involved with the development of the Pedigree and Whiskas Veterinary Diets range. His special interests are dietary management and communication. He now works for a healthcare advertising agency in London.

David Appleby is an animal behaviour counsellor based at the Pet Behaviour Centre, Upper St, Defford, Worcs WR8 9AB. Phone: 01386 750615; e-mail: appleby@petbcent.demon.co.uk. He is visiting pet behaviour counsellor at Cambridge University Veterinary School. He also holds clinics in Derby, Nottingham, Leicester, Northampton and Birmingham. He lectures at home and abroad on pet behaviour therapy and is a regular contributor to pet magazines. He is author of a series of behaviour booklets, stocked by vets' surgeries, including a guide to feline behaviour problems, *How to Have a Contented Cat*. He has appeared many times on TV and radio.

Evelyn Barbour-Hill, a veterinary surgeon in practice since 1972, has always been interested in the teeth and now spends the majority of his time treating the teeth, jaws and mouths of animals. In 1988 he founded the British Veterinary Dental Association with like-minded others and now serves as a spokesman for the association. He can be contacted at Tan y Coed, Penlon, High St, Bangor, North Wales LL57 IPX. Phone: 01248 355674.

Claire Bessant is Chief Executive of the Feline Advisory Bureau, a charity dedicated to the health and welfare of cats, which funds posts in feline medicine and produces advice leaflets. In 1996 she helped set up the European Society of Feline Medicine and is assistant editor of *The*

Journal of Feline Medicine and Surgery. She is editor of the *FAB Journal* and author of *How to Talk to Your Cat, The Ultrafit Older Cat*, and *Perfect Kitten*. She is an agony aunt for *Your Cat* magazine, answering questions on general cat care and cat behaviour.

John Foster is veterinary adviser to Friskies Pet Care, UK, and in practice at the Barton Veterinary Hospital, 34 New Dover Rd, Canterbury, Kent CT1 3DT. Phone: 01227 765522. His special interests include cat nutrition and ophthalmology.

David Godfrey is a partner in the Nine Lives Veterinary Practice for Cats. He is a Diplomate of the American Board of Veterinary Practitioners, certified in feline practice. He can be contacted at Nine Lives Veterinary Practice, 2068 Stratford Rd, Hockley Heath, West Midlands B94 6NT. Phone: 01564 782307; fax: 01564 785114; e-mail: nlvets@aol.com.

David Grant is a vet with the RSPCA and a former chief examiner for the Royal College of Veterinary Surgeons' Diploma in Veterinary Dermatology. He is author of *A Year in the Life of the Animal Hospital* and *Tales from the Animal Hospital* (Simon and Schuster).

Vicky Halls is a veterinary nurse and a cat behaviour counsellor at Lock View Cottage, Farleigh Lane, East Farleigh, Maidstone, Kent ME16 9LY. Phone: 01622 721845/0777 155 4282; e-mail: VickyHalls@aol.com. A member of the Association of Pet Behaviour Counsellors, she specializes in the complex study of feline behaviour problems. Her practice sees cases referred by vets throughout the south-east of England. She is a regular contributor to *All about Cats* magazine.

Anne Haughie is an expert in cat rescue and author of *The Feline Advisory Bureau Cat Rescue Manual*, a handbook of advice for would-be rescuers. She became involved in cat rescue in 1985, fostering cats and kittens for a small local organization and the RSPCA, before setting up a small purpose-built rescue facility in 1989. In 1996 she was elected on to the Feline Advisory Bureau Committee and has put together the FAB's Code of Practice for Rescue Facilities. She is working on a manual on feral cat management.

Sarah Heath is a vet and cat behaviour counsellor at 11 Cotebrook Drive, Upton, Chester CH2 1RA. Phone/fax: 01244 399228; e-mail: heath@vetethol.demon.co.uk. She is author of *Why Does My Cat . . . ?* (Bantam Books). She writes regularly for *Your Cat* and *Your Dog* magazines and lectures at home and abroad on pet behaviour therapy.

Emma Magnus is a consultant in animal behaviour based in East Anglia at 15 Parkwood, Henley Rd, Ipswich IPI 3SE. Phone: 01473 421886; fax: 01473 400601; mobile: 0421 062455; e-mail: emma@zoology.astra.co.uk. She is a member of the Association of Pet Behaviour Counsellors.

Simon Meyer is a vet with a special interest in feline medicine at 94 Dawes Rd, London SW6 7EJ (phone: 0171 381 3939; fax: 0171 385 6194) and 122 Glenthorne Rd, London W6 OLP (phone: 0181 748 9487; fax: 0181 746 3528).

Daniel Mills is a veterinary surgeon and lecturer in animal behaviour and welfare at De Montfort University, Lincoln's Caythorpe Campus, nr Grantham, Lincs NG32 3EP. From there he runs a behaviour clinic for companion animals (phone: 01400 275629; fax: 01400 275686; e-mail: dmills@dmu.ac.uk). He has written a range of scientific and popular papers on cat behaviour. He leads a research team which is focused on managing behaviour and understanding the personality of animals in order to improve their welfare. He is an adviser to several pet care companies and has spoken widely both in the UK and abroad on animal behaviour therapy and management. He is a founder member and currently Honorary Secretary of the Companion Animal Behaviour Therapy Study Group, which was set up to promote this field in a veterinary context.

Peter Neville, is a cat behaviour counsellor and can be contacted at PO Box 1735, Salisbury, Wilts SP2 0NG. Phone/fax: 01722 741440; e-mail: peter@cats-and-

143

dogs.freeserve.co.uk. He is a director of the Centre of Applied Pet Ethology and a chartered member of the Institute of Animal Care Education. He has lectured on pet behaviour in many countries including America, Japan and Argentina. He co-presented the video, *All You Need to Know About Cats* and is the originator of videos for pets including *Cool for Cats*. He has published many books and scientific publications, including the international bestseller *Do Cats Need Shrinks?*, *Claws and Purrs* and *The Perfect Kitten*.

Erica Peachey is a pet behaviour counsellor at 37 Lang Lane, West Kirby, Wirral, Merseyside L48 5HQ. Phone/fax: 0151 625 2568. She is the author of several dog booklets and sees clients in their own homes, at her practice or at behavioural clinics run from veterinary surgeries throughout the north of England. She gives seminars and courses at venues around the country, and talks at conferences and to dog training instructors, veterinary nurses and veterinary surgeons.

Caroline Prymak is a specialist in small animal surgery at the Centre for Small Animal Studies, the Animal Health Trust, Lanwades Park, Kentford, Newmarket CB8 7UU. She can also be consulted at Wey Referrals Woking, 125–9 Chertsey Rd, Woking, Surrey GU21 5BP and Ridgeway Referrals, 47 The Ridgeway, Flitwick, Bedfordshire MK45 1DJ. Caroline Prymak has a special interest in cancer surgery and pain relief in companion animals.

Ian Robinson graduated from the University of Durham in 1983 with a degree in zoology and obtained a PhD in animal behaviour from the University of Aberdeen in 1987. He joined the Waltham Centre for Pet Nutrition in 1988 to study the feeding behaviour of dogs and cats. Currently he is involved in studies of human–animal interactions, focusing on how both human and animal behaviour can influence the relationship and in particular how owners may derive health benefits from pet ownership. He is editor of *The Waltham Book of Human Animal Interaction: Benefits and Responsibilities of Pet Ownership*.

David Sands is senior animal psychologist at the Animal Behavioural Clinic, 148 Blackburn Rd, Heapey, Chorley, Lancs PR6 8EL. Phone/fax: 01257 249960; mobile: 0498 556598; e-mail: Dr_David_Sands@compuserve.com. He deals with a wide range of domesticated pet problems including unruly and un-housetrained cats. He has scripted a number of animal information videos on small animals, dogs and cats and has recently published three books in the *Caring for Pets* series, including *Cats and Kittens* (Salamander). He regularly contributes to UK TV and radio news programmes on related human and pet companionship subjects.

Bradley Viner qualified from the Royal Veterinary College in 1978 and set up his own small animal practice in Hatch End, Northwood, Bushey and Croxley Green on the outskirts of London. He spends a significant proportion of his time working with the media, having presented a weekly pet programme on LBC Radio for over ten years, writing for *Your Cat* magazine, and appearing regularly on television including on *Mad About Pets* for ITV, Granada's *This Morning* programme, and *Pets Go Public* for Channel 5. He writes a weekly column in *The People* newspaper. His books include *The Cat Care Manual*, *The Ultrafit Older Cat*, *Good Care for Dogs*, *The A–Z of Cat Care* and thirteen small books in the *All About Your Pet* series.

David Watson, a widely experienced vet, is Associate Editor with Veterinary Business Development, working on *Veterinary Times*, the *Veterinary Business Journal*, and other publications. Before this he worked for a pharmaceutical company and Pedigree Masterfoods. His special interests are pet care, nutrition and the relationships between people and their pets.

Sarah Whitehead is a member of the Association of Pet Behaviour Counsellors with a special interest in cats. A director of the Centre of Applied Pet Ethology, she runs several behavioural clinics, dealing with problems ranging from aggression to anxiety, as well as offering education courses to those interested in animal behaviour. She has authored, or co-authored, six books on

145

pet behaviour and is a regular contributor to many of the specialist pet magazines, TV and radio programmes. For a full list of books, videos and educational courses send an s.a.e. to COAPE, PO Box 18, Tisbury, Wilts SP3 6NQ.

Eric Wickham-Ruffle is a top judge of pedigree cats in Britain and around the world. He was for many years a member of the Executive Committee of the Governing Council of the Cat Fancy, and is one of the four Trustees in whom their property is vested. He is president or vice-president of many cat clubs including the Red Cream & Tortie Cat Society, the Kensington Kitten and Neuter Cat Club, the Blue Persian, the West of Scotland and the London Cat Club and others. He is co-author of *The Complete Persian* (Ringpress) and his *International Cat Encyclopaedia* will be published by Howells in 1999. For many years he was a leading breeder of chinchilla Persians.

Helpful Organizations

The Association of Pet Behaviour Counsellors, PO Box 46, Worcester WR8 9YS (phone: 01386 751151), can refer enquirers to their nearest cat behaviour counsellor. The association sells books and training items – send s.a.e. for catalogue. Consult the APBC website – www.apbc.org.uk – for a list of their members and the eighty-two clinics where they practise.

The British Veterinary Dental Association will assist any veterinary surgeon or animal owner with queries of a dental nature. They can refer enquirers to local veterinary surgeons who specialize in dentistry. Contact Evelyn Barbour-Hill, Tan y Coed, Penlon, High St, Bangor, North Wales LL57 IPX (phone: 01248 355674).

The Cats Protection League is Britain's largest and oldest cat charity. It is a cat rescue organization with 250 branches throughout the UK, who rescue and rehome about 75,000 cats a year. All the branches need fund-raisers, cat fosterers and volunteers, as well as money. The charity operates a neutering voucher scheme to help people in genuine need to neuter their cats. It also produces a range of very helpful leaflets on cat problems and cat care. Contact the CPL at 17 Kings Rd, Horsham, West Sussex RH13 5PN (helpline: 01403 221927).

The Feline Advisory Bureau, Taeselbury, High St, Tisbury, Wilts SP3 6LD, is a charity dedicated to the health and welfare of cats. It provides information on veterinary care and treatment of cats and organizes conferences, runs the *FAB Journal*, and publishes the *FAB Cat Rescue Manual*. It publishes fifty advice sheets on feline problems including a leaflet on choosing a good boarding cattery. It also publishes a list of good catteries and gives advice on quarantine catteries. FAB Helpline: 01747 871872; e-mail: fab.fab@ukonline.co.uk.

Pet Bereavement Helpline run by the Society for Companion Animal Studies. Ring 0800 0966606 for details.

The Royal Society for the Prevention of Cruelty to Animals, The Causeway, Horsham, West Sussex RH12 1HG (phone: 01403 264181) is Britain's major Pet rescue charity. Its branches rescue and rehome unwanted animals. Its inspectors investigate all reports of animal cruelty. If you report a case of cruelty to cats, they will not reveal your identity. The RSPCA Cruelty Hotline is 0990 555999.

Useful Products

Fat Cats, Faddy Cats
Cat aerobic centres can be ordered through pet shops. If you have difficulty, contact Canac Pet Products, Becks Mill, Westbury Leigh, Westbury, Wilts BA13 3SD.

Raised feeding bowls are available from Luxway Canine Supplies, Brabourne Lees, Ashford, Kent TN25 5LG. (phone: 01303 812440).

CET toothpaste, toothbrushes and dental treats are sold in vets' surgeries or under the name Petrodex in pet shops.

Hills prescription diet Feline t/d is for cats prone to gingivitis. Hills Helpline: 0800 282438.

Sex, Hatred, Sibling Rivalry

Feliway Natural Spray, made by Sanofi, is similar to a cat's facial pheromones and is obtainable on prescription from a vet. It must be used strictly according to its instructions.

Staywell electronic pet doors are sold through pet shops and DIY stores. If you have difficulty finding them, phone 01772 793793.

Litter Training, Litter Troubles

For an allergic cat, try Natural Friendly Cat Litter available by mail order from 01302 700220 (Old House Farm, Stubbs Walden, Doncaster DN6 9BU). Or Bio-Catolet litter, Midas Products Ltd, PO Box 855, Buckingham, MK18 3ZQ (phone: 01296 714000).

To teach your cat to use the lavatory, try the Kitty Whizz Transfer System – Voy-Toys Inc., 400 So. 5th St, Harrison, NM 07029, USA (phone: 201 484 0088).

The self-cleaning litter tray is Littermaid, available from Comtrad Industries, 2820 Waterford Lake Drive, Suite 106, Midlothian, Virginia 23113, USA. Its internet site is http://www.littermaid.com.

Purrfitz disposable litter trays are available from pet shops and made by Interpet, Vincent Lane, Dorking, Surrey RH4 3YX (phone: 01306 881033).

The Petfresh Cat Litter House is sold by mail order from Petfresh Products, Salthill Lodge, Salthill Lane, Chichester PO19 3AX (phone: 01243 785024).

Wandering Cats, Indoor Cats

For microchipping – Petlog, PO Box 2037, London W1A 1GP. This register is supported by the RSPCA.

Home-made safety collars cost £1.50 (1999 prices) plus a stout s.a.e. from Grace Officer, 13 Hall Close, Farncombe, Godalming, Surrey GU7 3PW.

Radio transmitters, receivers and directional antennae from Biotrack Ltd, 52 Furzebrook Rd, Wareham, Dorset BH20 5AX (phone: 01929 552992).

Cat aerobic centres can be ordered through pet shops. See under *Chapter Two*, above.

Renardine animal deterrent and Rencoco mulch, made of cocoa-bean shells with renardine, are obtainable from Roebuck-Eyot, 7A Hatfield Way, Bishop Auckland, County Durham DL14 6XF (phone: 01388 772233).

Balding Cats, Furballs, Feline Coiffure

Flea treatments, Frontline, Advantage, Program, are available on prescription from a vet.

Household flea products include Vetkem Acclaim, Zodiac household spray, Canovel Pet Bedding, Flego and Micro-Shield High Performance.

Bob Martin's Cod Liver Conditioning Oil is sold through supermarkets and pet shops.

Efapet coat conditioner and Efapet problem skin relief are sold in supermarkets and pet shops. Efamol Information Line: 0870 6060128.

Katalax or Johnson's Hairball Remedy help with fur balls.

Old Age and the Last Goodbye

Cozee Comfort heated pads, "electric blankets for pets", are available from Burco Dean Appliances Ltd, Rosegrove, Burnley, Lancs BB12 6AL (phone: 01282 422851).

Petliners, absorbent paper mats and rolls, can be ordered on 01405 831003.

Acknowledgments

This book could not have been compiled without the help of many readers of the *Daily Telegraph*. The cat owners and correspondents who kindly gave permission to publish their letters include:

Heather Adlam, Anita Allen, Pauline Andrews, Susan Archer, Daniel Arden, Norah Austin, Margaret Ayrton, Emma Baatz, Audrey Barry, B.D. Barton, Diana Baum, Martin Bean, Margaret R. Bellard, Mary Best, Gill Box, Liz Boys, A.E. Bricem, Judith Brindley, Norma Brinsden, L. Bunbury, John Bunting, Lillian Burden, Mary Burrows, R.A. Caulton, David Chatfield, Pat Cheese, Pauline Chilton, Hilary Clare, Joanne Colthrup, Alison Cookson, J. Cooper, Joan Corbel, D. Critten, E. Curnow, Shirley Davey, Eira Davies, Sally Dearling, Jill

Dennis, Alice Donovan, Sally Donovan, Janice Downes, Pauline Drury, P.A. Duff, Gillian Duncan, M. Evans, Fiona Fairbairn, J. Fairbrother, Susan Farr, Caroline Fletcher, Robin Flood, Nora Ford, Avril Fuhrmann, Patricia Gallimore, Mary Gibson, Doreen Glynn, Fran Godfrey, James Graham, C. Gray, Audrey Green, Wendy Gregory, Derek Gritten, Valerie Grose, Michèle Gross, Issidy Hafner, Graham Hall, Marjorie Hall, Peter Hall, Diana Hamblen, E. Hampard, S. Harris, Dee Hartland-Swann, L. Haycock, Victoria Head, Barbara Hindley, D. Hook, Linda Howe, G.W. Howell, A. Howlett, David Hunter, Mary Hyde, Nancy Imlay, M. Irven, Mary Jackson, Barbara de Jager, Helen Johnson, Anne Johnstone, Katherine Kantolinna, Martin Karmel, Gabrielle Kennedy, A.R. Knott, F.C. Knowles, K. Littlechild, Jane Lockyer, Patricia Lodge, Joy Lowe, Clare Lund, Doreen Mackie, Miriam Manning, Laurie Manton, Rosemary Marshall, Hilary Martson, Enid Marten, Pat Mattinson, Gillian McCallan, George McGeachie, J. Mckenna, Stevie McLinden, Chloe Milton, Pat Milton, Beryl Mingham, Jean Mitchener, Rosemary Moor, Corenne and Colin Morgan, Veronica Moseley, D. Mullen, Rosalind Murray, Sheila Naish, Joan Nelson, David Neville, Leslie Orton, Marjorie Ostler, Jenny Papadopoulos, Mary Parkinson, P. Payne, Christine Peake, V.T. Percy, D.M. Perkins, Purrette Price, Winifred Pringle, S. Puckett, Coral Ragoni, Patrick Rangecroft, Gillian Richardson, Martin Roberts, Ian Robertson, Margaret Robertson, Margaret Rogers, J. Routledge, Marjorie Rowe, Anne Rudd, Maggie Russell, Sally Sandy, C. Seager, John and Maureen Seccombe, John Shellard, Cherril Shepherd, Penny Sheridan, John Sherrard, Jean Shorter, I.R. Stephen, Kathleen Stevens, Judy Stringer, Sylvia Swain, Diana Symon, H. Tanner, B. Taylor, Maureen Taylor, Richard Taylor, Dinah Thomas, Julie Turner, Evelyn Tyrer, Heather Wake, Elizabeth Walters, Jill Ward, J. Watson, Julie Western, Mairead West-Oram, P. White, Maurice and Brenda Wilde, Carol Wilson, Daphne Wilson, Jan Wise, S. Wood, Roger Woodall, Jane Woodbury-Eggins, John Yeowell, Elaine Young.

Every effort has been made by the author to contact each

individual contributor. If any letter has appeared without proper acknowledgment, the author, the publishers and the *Daily Telegraph* apologize unreservedly. Please address any queries to the editor, c/o the publishers.

Index